Wednesday
is for Witch

With special thanks to Anna McKerrow

First published in Great Britain in 2023 by Wren & Rook

ISBN: 978 1 5263 6633 7

1 3 5 7 9 10 8 6 4 2

Wren & Rook
An imprint of
Hachette Children's Group
Part of Hodder & Stoughton
Carmelite House
50 Victoria Embankment
London EC4Y 0DZ

An Hachette UK Company
www.hachette.co.uk
www.hachettechildrens.co.uk

Printed and bound in Great Britain by Clays Ltd, Elcograf S.p.A.

Wednesday is for Witch

A Spell a Day for Good Witch Vibes

LYRA PENROSE

wren
&rook

Introduction

*W*elcome *to your very own introduction to the world of spells and witchcraft.*

If you have ever felt like there is magic in you – some call it intuition – but you didn't know how to make it flourish, then this book is for you. If you want more magic in your day-to-day life, then allow this book to be your guide. And if you're looking for simple and fun ways to boost your well-being, then read on...

Today's young witches are exploring the opportunities for self-care that magic provides. Just like straight-talking Wednesday Addams, you know your own mind, are kind to yourself and are committed to manifesting your destiny, whether that involves visualisation, positive affirmations, mindfulness or even casting a magic spell or two.

Wednesday is for Witch contains a spell, ritual or affirmation for every day of the year. You can start at the beginning and work your way through each week, or dip in and out and pick the spells that resonate with you on any given day. All the spells are ethical and created for good witch vibes only.

Within these pages, you can safely explore crystal spells, ask the moon to manifest your wishes, use everyday items from around the house in simple rituals or just enjoy a magical bath to soothe away your worries. Whether you're exploring witchcraft for the first time or want something easy that doesn't require lots of complicated equipment, *Wednesday is for Witch* holds the key to your deepest wishes.

Lastly, whilst Wednesday is no stranger to a little light revenge, do remember that you should only perform spells and rituals for good. The karmic law, which all good witches abide by, states that when you wish bad luck on another it is likely to return to you threefold – yes, that's three times the bad luck! Be mindful of this as your witch powers blossom.

A note on health and safety

Some of these spells suggest burning candles and incense – please bear in mind that candles and incense once lit must never be left unattended. If you're not an adult, always ask your chief witch or wizard if it's OK to use them in the house.

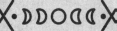

Week 1

Monday

An altar for infinite magic

Before you cast a spell, you need to prepare an altar. This is a safe and sacred space to perform your spells. You could use a bedside table, a windowsill or even make a portable altar so you can perform spells anytime the mood takes you.

In order to help summon and harness the forces of nature, the four elements – earth, air, fire and water – should be represented. There are many ways they can be included, for instance you could use a tea light candle and matches for fire, a feather or incense stick in a holder for air, a crystal or pine cone to represent earth and a small, filled receptacle, such as a cup, glass or mug, for water. An image of the pentagram – the five -pointed star that is the witch's symbol of magic and protection – is also needed.

Pentagram

Put them all together on a surface and you are ready to make magic. To make a portable altar, find a nice bag to put all your bits in and take it with you when you're out and about, in case the need for magic strikes!

Tuesday

A protection talisman for your bedroom

Make a pentagram to hang above your door for protection and to attract good witch energy. Four of the star's points represent one of the elements each, the fifth point represents the spirit. The pentagram symbol should always be present when casting spells. Make your own pentagram by gathering five twigs of a similar length picked up on a walk (only use 'windfall' wood that has already dropped from the tree and always ask for the blessings of the trees before you take it), then tie together with string. Add a loop of string to hang it up either beside your altar or an entry point to the place where you intend to cast your spells.

Wednesday

A ritual to prepare for spell-casting

Your altar and precious objects provide the structure to direct your thoughts and energies to manifest a spell into reality, but an open mind is key to successful witchcraft. A grounding ritual is the best way to prepare your mind for magic – you won't get anywhere with a head crammed full of other things you should be doing instead.

Begin by casting a safe circle around you with your index finger, using a clockwise motion – imagine the circle as white light – then step inside the safe circle. This is your sacred space where you will conduct your magic. Ideally, your altar will be within the circle, but do what you can with the space you have. Trace the circle with each element in turn: with the feather or lit incense for air, with the candle for fire, with the cup of water for water and with a pentacle (a magical, five-pointed talisman) or a crystal for earth. In your mind's eye, see the circle of white light surround you and contain you, above and below the ground.

Now, call on the four elements to be with you in the circle. Face east and hold out your hands, saying firmly, 'I call to the powers of air to be with me in my rite, may you lend me your qualities of clarity, inspiration and speed.'

Now face south and say, 'I call to the powers of fire to be with me in my rite, may you lend me your qualities of creativity, power and enthusiasm.'

Now face west and say, 'I call to the powers of water to be with me in my rite, may you lend me your qualities of healing, sensitivity and psychic awareness.'

Now face north and say 'I call to the powers of earth to be with me in my rite, may you lend me your qualities of stability, abundance and fertility.'

When you have called all four elements in, do your ritual.

When you feel ready, thank the elemental powers one by one for attending your ritual, and banish the circle. You can do this simply by imagining the sphere of light going back into the earth. Make sure that you say 'I bid you hail and farewell' to each of the elements as you close the circle, and where you worked clockwise to call the elements in, banish them in a counterclockwise order: north, west, south, east.

Thursday

Mantra magic!

Mantras are powerful affirmations you can say to yourself to call your hopes and dreams into existence. Speak it, believe it and live it. Look in the mirror and repeat five times:

I believe in my infinite potential!

Friday

Abracadabra luck spell

This abracadabra spell has been used since the third century BCE to heal minor ailments and bring luck to the receiver of the spell. The eleven letters represent eleven days until the luck reaches optimum power or an ailment goes away. Write out ABRACADABRA on a piece of paper and then continue writing the word underneath, taking out a letter every time, so it looks like this, below. Give the spell to the person that it is intended for – they must keep it with them for eleven days for the magic to work.

ABRACADABRA
ABRACADABR
ABRACADAB
ABRACADA
ABRACAD
ABRACA
ABRAC
ABRA
ABR
AB
A

Saturday

Bath ritual for self-love

Taking a bath is one of the simplest and most powerful ways to perform magic and connect with nature. Try a few drops of vanilla, sandalwood, lavender, neroli or ylang-ylang essential oils in your bath to calm your mind and soothe away worries and self-doubt. Choose whichever oil smells good to you. Arrange some small pieces of rose quartz around the edge of your bath and add tea light candles (if you have them). Once in the bath, close your eyes and repeat to yourself: 'I am loved. I am beautiful. I am supported in everything I do.'

Sunday

Mantra magic!

Repeat three times in preparation for the week ahead:

I am a powerful force for good

Week 2

Monday

Red letter spell

If you want a swift answer to a question that has been playing on your mind, get yourself a ripe apple and a peeler and start peeling! Try to peel off the skin in one continuous strand, or as much as you can manage, then throw the peel over your left shoulder. The peel should land in a position that will represent a letter of the alphabet which will provide you with an important clue to answering your question. Victorians used this method to predict the name of their future love, but you could use this simple ritual for anything that needs an initial as an answer.

Tuesday

Mindful walk ritual

Mindfulness is the practice of focusing your awareness on the present moment and is a technique that has proven to promote calm and happiness, as well as giving your mental and physical well-being a boost.

When you're next out for a walk, use your senses to awaken your witch energies and feel present. Begin by noticing the sensation of the fresh air against your face, the warmth of the sun or the coolness of the rain. Notice the ground as you walk and the sound of your footsteps. Inhale the smells, notice the sounds and enjoy the feelings of natural textures of stone, tree bark or leaves against your skin. Stay in the moment, simply noticing and feeling these sensations.

Wednesday

Primrose tea for calm

Primrose is well known for its calming properties and primrose tea will hit the spot when you need to relax. Begin by foraging for fresh yellow primrose flowers – they flower from January to May in the northern hemisphere – a handful will do the trick. Wash the petals and place in a teapot and cover in boiling water. Steep for a few minutes and pour into a cup, using a strainer to catch the petals. Relax and enjoy your soothing tea. You can make this a little ritual at bedtime when you have a big day coming up.

Thursday

Mantra magic!

Repeat these words three times as you stir your morning coffee:

There is magic all around me

Friday

Hag stone spell

Next time you're on a pebbly beach, hunt for a stone with a hole all the way through the middle. These are called holey stones or hag stones and are believed to protect the owner from curses. Some witches believe that if you look through the hole, you will see through any bad magic or illusions. If you find a hag stone, keep it and place it on your windowsill or by your door at home to protect your space. You could also keep it in your pocket as a protective talisman, or if it's small enough, thread it on to a necklace so you can see through any lies that you are being told.

Saturday

Bibliomancy ritual

Take a meander through a bookshop or library and pick up a book at random. Now, close your eyes and ask the book a question that you're desperate to know the answer to. Open the book at any page and run your finger down the page until it feels right. The line you have marked with your finger contains your answer.

Sunday

Mantra magic!

Repeat these words with conviction:

I am a powerful witch

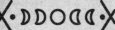

Week 3

Monday

Black mirror scrying

A black mirror is a traditional tool in witchcraft used for 'scrying', which is an ancient term for fortune-telling. Who doesn't want to get a glimpse of what's to come? You can make a black mirror simply by painting the back of a smooth piece of glass or a piece of clear acrylic (don't use anything with a sharp or jagged edge) with black paint. You can find acrylic at a craft shop or use the glass from a picture frame. This creates a blank surface that, when you stare into it for a long period of time, can act as a canvas for psychic messages. You might see flashes of colour and distinct shapes or receive messages in your mind containing seemingly random dream-like pictures or memories. Trust whatever comes, write down your results and consider their significance. Give it a try!

Tuesday

How to listen to messages from the universe

Another window into the future is to notice the messages that appear as you go about your day. For example, you might keep seeing the same word, number or image multiples times. Is this a message that is meaningful to you in some way? Adverts on TV, social media and even posters on the side of the road can all carry hidden messages for you.

Wednesday

Phone screen scrying spell

You might not have realised this, but you have a black mirror in your possession already, because your blank phone screen is a modern-day black mirror! Use it in the traditional way by sitting quietly, connecting to your intuition and staring into the blank, switched-off screen. Try not to think about anything in particular and see what images come to you: you might see anything from shapes and colours to pictures in your mind, or you might even find yourself humming a particular song. What these images, sounds or thoughts mean to you will be personal, so think about what those things mean to you. You could also investigate common colour associations, or things such as the meanings of particular spirit animals, or the magical meanings of plants or certain shapes, if you see those. Practise using the screen in this way regularly, noting down the results, and research anything that doesn't make immediate sense to you.

Thursday

Mantra magic!

Repeat these words before you rush out the door in the morning:

I am in control of my destiny

Friday

Look-up ritual

Take a walk outside on a dry day and find a quiet spot in a park or garden. Lie on your back and stare up at the clouds. Quieten your mind and relax your body. What images do you see in the cloud formations? There are no right or wrong answers here, just notice what you see and maybe do some research about what those symbols might be telling you.

Saturday

Wise moon spell

Step outside on a clear night and bathe yourself in moonlight, whatever the moon's phase. Feel yourself connect with the moon's positive energy and ask her to gift you with her wisdom. Close your eyes and be open to the messages or images that come to you.

Sunday

Mantra magic!

If you're feeling the Sunday evening blues, repeat three times:

I trust in the universe's plan for me

Week 4

Monday

Dream scrying

Get into the habit of writing down your dreams when you wake up in the morning, before you forget them. Keep a notebook and pen by your bed to make this easier. Once you have started remembering your dreams, write down a specific question you want an answer to and put it under your pillow. Go to sleep thinking of the question. When you wake up, note down your dreams. Did you receive an answer?

Tuesday

Enchanted pen spell

To bless your writing with eloquence, take your favourite pen and place it on your altar on a Tuesday when the moon is waxing (that is, when it's between 'half' and 'full'). Trace the symbol for the planet Mercury (you can find this below) over your pen with incense smoke to represent the air element, then use a lit candle for fire, a wet finger from your cup for water, then use a crystal or stone to trace the symbol to represent earth. Ask Mercury – traditionally associated with communication, speed, wit and writing – to bless you with excellent communication and writing skills.

Astrological symbol for Mercury

Wednesday

Dream scrying with a vision board

Make a simple image using collage, or use your own artistic skills, that represents intuition or being psychic. This can be anything you like, but it could feature the moon, a witchy image that resonates with you, a crystal ball, tarot cards, stars, special symbols or sacred animals. Put the image at the end of your bed and look at it for ten minutes before going to sleep. Go to sleep with the intention that your dreams, with the aid of your vision board, will help develop your intuition.

Thursday

Mantra magic!

Repeat three times and see what the day brings:

I am walking the road to success

Friday

Feather scrying spell

Feathers are often considered messages from the universe, especially if you find one in an unusual place. The message might be that you are loved or protected, or that your spells are working.

Feathers can also be used as part of an easy scrying spell. First, find one you like, and bless it with the four elements on your altar. Ask each element in turn to cleanse and bless the feather – pass it through incense smoke, sprinkle it with water, hold it near (but a safe distance away) the candle flame and touch it with a crystal or stone. Then, hold the feather above your head and focus on a question you want to ask about the future. Finally, let the feather go. If it lands on your left, the answer is no. If it lands on your right, the answer is yes. If it falls in the middle, you can repeat the process. If the feather falls in the middle again, the universe isn't ready to answer your question right now – or, it might not be an easy yes or no answer.

Saturday

Fire scrying ritual

If you are attending a bonfire or have one in your garden, get in a meditative mood and stare into the flames. Relax and let yourself see pictures in your mind's eye. You could ask a question before you begin, or just be open to what comes. If you would like to make it a bit more formal, you could say something like, 'Blessings to you, spirits of fire. Thank you for your wisdom and for attending my rite. Please lend me your insight, creativity and warmth and fuel my visions with your fiery power,' before you start. After you have meditated quietly on the fire, thank the fire spirits by saying, 'Thank you, fire spirits, for your vision and inspiration. I bid you farewell.'

Sunday

Mantra magic!

Repeat three times to draw positivity to you:

Laughter, light and love surround me always

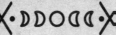

Week 5

Monday

Stormy moods spell

This spell harnesses the power of a storm to drive away your anger. Only go out in a storm if it is safe to do so, consider the reasons for your anger and shout them into the storm. Allow the storm to absorb your upsets and carry them away. On a quieter day, try blowing bubbles into the air and watching them float away with your worries.

Tuesday

Fancy-feather scrying ritual

Go for a walk with the intention you will find a feather that has a special meaning for you. When you find one, try to identify which bird it might have come from and look up the qualities associated with that bird. Feathers in general can be messages from the universe or symbols for protection or messages from angels. Different colour feathers represent different things:

Grey feathers represent
wisdom and the
pursuit of knowledge

Brown and red feathers
represent energy
and strength

Yellow feathers represent
joy and positivity

Black feathers can be a
warning to protect your peace
or work on your well-being

White feathers symbolise
that someone is thinking
about you and cares for
your happiness

Wednesday

Sweet wrapper enchantment spell

Collect colourful sweet wrappers and place them into a clear glass bottle or jar with a secure lid. Every time you add in a new wrapper, say thank you for something good in your life. When the bottle or jar is completely full and the wrappers are really packed in, secure the lid and carefully drip wax to seal the bottle. Display your bottle or jar in a favourite spot to attract good vibes into your life.

Thursday

Mantra magic!

Repeat three times whenever you need a bit of a boost:

I make magic happen

Friday

Magazine oracle spell

Pick up a magazine from a shop. Close your eyes and ask a burning question. Open the magazine to a random page and see what wisdom is available for you there.

Saturday

Sun strength spell

Go out on a sunny day and stand in direct sunlight (remember to wear SPF!). Close your eyes and feel the sun warm your body. Imagine the sun's light and heat penetrating your physical body and filling it up with strength, like you're a battery being filled with power. Repeat the mantra below, until you feel full of sun energy.

I am sun, I am strong

Sunday

4. 2/24

Mantra magic!

Always remember this:

Laughter, light and love surround me now

Week 6

5.2.24
Monday

Sea spell

The sea carries immense power and energy and is governed by the moon's cycles, just like us humans, so it's no surprise that we feel an affinity for it. On a clear and calm day, go to the sea and ask it a question. Paddle into the water a little, enjoy the feel of the water and the sand beneath your feet and listen for an answer. Close your eyes and be open to whatever message or image comes to you.

6.2.24
Tuesday

Rosemary cleansing spell

Rosemary has been used since ancient times to ward off evil energies and spirits and dispel negativity. For this spell, begin by gathering a couple of sprigs of fresh rosemary, put it into a small muslin or fabric bag and hang it from the shower head. When you turn the shower on, make sure that the warm water is running through the bag, infusing your shower with cleansing magic. Imagine the shower water washing negativity away. Imagine worry, pain and sadness running from you and down the drain. When you feel cleansed and purified, dry off with a clean towel and feel lovely for the rest of the day!

Wednesday

Clear-air breath spell

To release negative thoughts about yourself, stand in front of your altar. Light a white candle and some incense. Connect to the earth by imagining your feet growing roots into the ground. Then, imagine a silver thread attaching the top of your head to the light of the moon. Now, focus on your breathing and imagine a protective white light encircling you and dissolving your negative thoughts. Blow out the candle and say:

I'm free of negativity,
Free to be me,
So mote it be!

The final line is a common witchy phrase, and simply means 'So be it'.

Thursday

Mantra magic!

Call to the moon three times:

I am blessed by the moon

Friday

Money tree spell

If you're short of cash, gather some ribbon or strips of material and tie them to a tree's branches and make a wish for money to come to you. As you tie each strip of material or ribbon to the tree, say:

Money tree, money tree,
Send money onto me.

Tie your ribbon tight enough that it stays on, but not so tight that it harms the tree. You could also add small bells, beads or other little treasures to the ribbon before you tie it on.

Saturday

Oat bath ritual for good skin and good vibes

Oats are very good for dry and itchy skin, and oats are also well known for boosting strength, fortifying the body and dispelling sadness. Fill an old (clean!) sock with dry porridge oats and hook it over the hot tap. Turn the tap on and let the water strain through the oats in the sock, giving you a lovely milky oat bath.

Sunday

Mantra magic!

Say this in earnest to your reflection in the mirror:

I care for myself; I love myself; I value myself

Week 7

Monday

Exercise ritual

Start the week right with an exercise ritual to focus both mind and body. At the beginning of whatever exercise you do, set an intention: it could be for greater strength and vitality, a boost to your immune system or to simply look great. If you can, put a clear quartz crystal in your pocket as you exercise or hold it in your hand for some of your workout. With each movement, visualise achieving your intention. When you've finished, keep the crystal with you: it's now charged with positive energy for when you require it.

Tuesday

Simple coffee grounds reading

Make a cup of coffee using ground coffee (not instant) in a cafetiere and pour yourself a cup. Think of a burning question that you would like an answer to and mull it over as you drink your coffee. When you reach the coffee grounds at the bottom of the cup, turn your cup upside down on to a saucer or small plate and allow the coffee grounds to drop on to it. Ask your question out loud and then lift the cup. Now look at the shapes that the grounds have created and see what silhouettes they resemble. You can look up common meanings for shapes and symbols online. Some of the most common ones include:

Anchor: happy in love
Apples: exam success
Fish: news from a friend
Heart: healing and good times
Ladder: travel
Mountain: help from a mentor
Scissors: disagreements
Snake: dishonesty
Triangle: money luck
Unicorns: unexpected news

Wednesday <u>14/2/2024</u>

Points in time coffee reading

Some people believe that the teacup should be seen as divided into three 'zones' for fortune telling: the rim symbolises the present, the sides are the near future and the bottom of the cup represents the far future. You might like to ask about how to best look after yourself now and in the future, what will happen with your studies or a particular friendship or even your career. Tap into your intuition to see what the shapes formed by the leaves might be telling you.

Thursday

Mantra magic!

Call this mantra into the night sky:

Above me, stars; below me, earth; within me, magic!

Friday

Bubble bath ritual for happiness

If you're feeling low, try soaking in a happiness bath! Pick some petals in bright colours, then draw a bubble bath and add a few drops of orange or grapefruit oil to the water. Sprinkle the petals in the bath while saying:

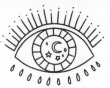

I am happy, I am joyful

Once you have finished your soak, scoop up the petals, press them in between two sheets of newspaper and weigh down with books. When the petals are dry and pressed (usually after a week or two) write down your hopes and wishes on them and keep them on your altar.

Saturday

Fire banishing spell

Stand before your altar and light a candle and some incense. Any type of incense is fine, but so-called Dragon's Blood is especially good for banishing.

Write the thing you wish to be rid of on a bay leaf, place it on the image of a pentagram in the centre of your altar and say these words eight times:

Spirits of the elements,
Banish my problem,
So mote it be!

Meditate on your problem being washed away with water, burnt away with fire, covered in earth and blown away by the wind. Finally, put your bay leaf into a safe, heat-proof bowl or dish and burn it.

Sunday

Mantra magic!

You're doing so well with your spell-craft, always remember:

Every spell teaches me something new

Week 8

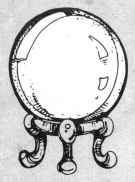

Monday

Banish bad vibes spell

If you've had a run of bad luck or generally feel that the universe isn't on your side, here's a spell to clear away bad vibes. Take a compact mirror and place it on your windowsill, with the mirror facing out the window. Now, light a small tea light candle on your altar, and repeat the words:

I send back the bad vibes.
Good witch vibes only shall
pass through these walls.
So mote it be!

Once you've said it, watch the candle flame dance and imagine white light filling your room. Now blow out the candle but leave the mirror in place until the next new moon.

Tuesday

Cloud-busting spell

If you feel worried, go to your altar and light some incense, which represents air. Look out of the window at the sky and imagine your worries are the clouds. Now, watch as they get blown around and dissipated by the wind (this spell works best in autumn and winter!). Feel your worries being blown away, and softly blow air into the incense smoke too, watching it move and melt away. Know that you have the power to control your worries.

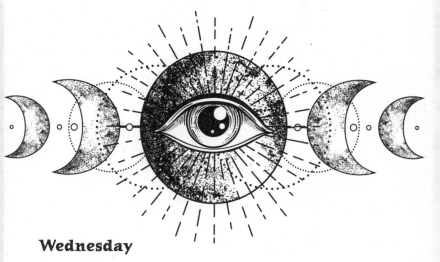

Wednesday

Flower spell

Research the meaning of flowers and select a type that represents something you want to attract into your life. Gather or purchase your chosen flowers and display them somewhere prominent in your home where you (and anyone else you live with!) can enjoy them and their magical properties. Some examples of the magical associations of flowers include:

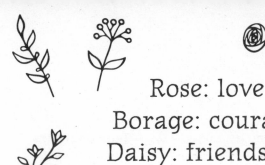

Rose: love
Borage: courage
Daisy: friendship
Carnation: beauty
Geranium: positive energy
Chrysanthemum: protection
Clover: abundance
Dahlia: wisdom

Thursday

Mantra magic!

Say with conviction:

I can achieve whatever I focus on

Friday

Running spell

When you're running, imagine you are running towards what you want and leaving behind what you don't. It's a very simple and active way to visualise reaching your goals and leaving behind your worries, as well as a great way of doing some physical magic and directing your body's energy towards your aims.

Saturday

Paperclips magic circle

To make a mini magic ring as part of a portable altar while you're out and about, link paperclips together to form a circle. The more paperclips you have, the bigger the circle. Simple and efficient!

Sunday

Mantra magic!

I attract beautiful abundance in all areas of my life

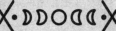

Week 9

Monday

Lunchbox spell

Add some extra yum to everything in your lunchbox by saying a little spell over it under the light of the full moon. Place your hands on the lunchbox and chant:

Magic spice,
Let my lunch be extra nice!

Tuesday

Post-its protection spell

Draw a pentagram on the sticky side of a post-it note and stick it to your mobile phone so that the pentagram is facing the screen. This will act as protection for your online interactions.

Wednesday

Glue stick spell

Cut out a selection of images that represent your goals
for the future – no matter how big or small. Perhaps you
want to travel or get an internship, meet new friends,
learn a new skill or achieve your personal best in your
favourite sport. Use a glue stick to make a little collage
of the images. Keep the image on your altar and look at
it every day as a daily reminder of your goals.

9/2/24 ## Thursday

Mantra magic!

I achieve every goal I set

Friday

Glitter-magic sparkle spell

If you have a glitter ink pen, use it to write your spells for
extra magic and sparkle. If you have more than one, use
different colours for different spells: purple for boosting
psychic ability, silver for moon spells, gold for success,
pink for friendship, green for abundance and blue for
luck.

Saturday

Key to good luck spell

Find an old key no-one needs. Write I AM LUCKY on a piece of paper and bind it to the key with red thread or wool. Find a crossroads (where three or more roads meet) and leave your key somewhere hidden.

Sunday

Mantra magic!

I create my own reality

Week 10

Monday

The witch's wand

Your wand can be as simple or as fancy as you want. If it has meaning for you, a discarded branch from a tree could be it. You can keep the branch au naturel or shape it into something more like a traditional wand shape. Try carefully stripping off the bark and sanding or whittling the wand into whatever shape and texture you like. Any wood is fine to use if you feel drawn to it, but some particularly witchy types are rowan, apple, oak, ash, birch or hawthorn. As with all witchy tools, you can find some fancy ones online or in witchy shops, but you don't need anything expensive. A magic wand can focus your energy to a particular object and charge it with magical intention. It is also useful for casting a protective circle before spell-casting.

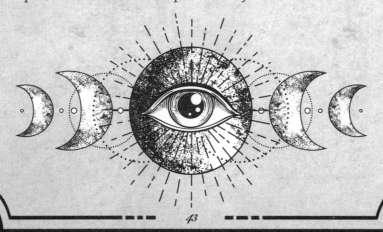

Tuesday

Eraser 'rub-it-out' spell

Write down something that is bothering you in pencil on a piece of paper. Now, mindfully rub it out with your eraser. As you do, say the following words ten times:

I erase this problem!

Wednesday

Water bottle thankfulness spell

When you're out walking, pour some water from your water bottle at the base of a tree or a plant you pass, and stop and say a little thank you to nature for its abundance. The more you say thank you to the universe, the more you will attract good things your way.

Thursday

Mantra magic!

My words and thoughts are powerful

Friday

Putting the 'craft' in witchcraft spell

Make some pencil drawings of plants you see in your local area, in your house, garden or outside your window. Identify the plants and their magical uses and keep the drawings safe for when you might need them for spell-casting. Some examples of plants and their magic properties include:

Lavender: for calm and new love
Sage: to banish bad vibes
Clove: to stop gossip
Fern: to disperse stormy moods
Dill: to help nurture new ideas

Saturday

Hair band 'keep us together' spell

To help a friendship stay strong, use a hair band to bind two pebbles that you might find on a beach or in a park. Visualise one pebble being you and the other being your friend. This should only be used with the consent of your friend – perhaps in the event of potentially being split up in some way.

Sunday

Mantra magic!

I transform myself
with magic

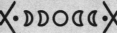

Week 11

Monday

Little treasure prosperity spell

On a full moon, find four small items you're fond of but don't mind giving away, such as a key ring, a little toy, a hair tie, a pretty stone or a shell. Hold them in your hands, one by one, and pour all your love into them. Set them on your altar to absorb the full moon vibes. The next day, leave them outside in places they can be found by others (on a wall, in a field, on a park bench, etc.). You are giving gifts to the universe so that it will give gifts to you. Try it!

Tuesday

Key ring witch spell

An easy way to have a little bit of magic and protection with you at all times is to make a pentagram key ring and add it to your keys. You could try making one from stiff card and laminating it, or by gluing some matches together and spray-painting them silver or gold. Perhaps even crochet a pentagram if you're feeling especially crafty! Whatever you make, charge it on your altar among all four elements when it's finished. Hold your keys and the key ring in your hands and say:

Magic keys,
Magic keys,
Keep my keys
safe, please!

Wednesday

Travel well spell

Under the light of a full moon, hold your travel pass (whatever kind you have) between your hands. Feel the power of the moon entering the top of your head and glowing through your body, into your hands. Feel the earth's energy coming up through your feet and merging in your middle. Draw the shape of a pentagram over your travel pass with your finger and ask all your travel with it to be blessed, protected, pleasant and swift.

Thursday

Mantra magic!

Magic flows through me

Friday

Money bag spell

Your purse or wallet is an excellent place to keep a little magic bag spell. On a new moon, take a small fabric bag with a drawstring top. Add to it a bay leaf and a citrine crystal to draw money and abundance to you. Tuck the little bag into your purse.

Saturday

Pop tart spell

Write your wish on a pop tart with a non-toxic pen, or carve the words carefully with a pin, then toast the pop tart and eat it (writing on plain toast will also work). You can also empower yourself by drawing magical symbols on your toast and eating that – use squirty jam for added fun! This spell will work for any simple manifesting aim.

Sunday

Mantra magic!

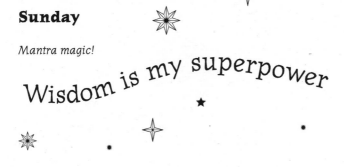

Wisdom is my superpower

Week 12

Monday

Bullet journal: moon phases

Begin a magical bullet journal. This is a cross between an art project, a planner and a diary. Write and draw pretty, themed pages in a journal recording the different phases of the moon. Use colour, paint and glitter, and really go to town drawing the moon phases, making a page of information about how long each phase lasts, as well as the different names for them. You might like to create some new moon, full moon and dark moon mantras to use and write them in your bullet journal, too. Some suggestions might be:

I am filled with the potential of the new moon,

I feel the power of the full moon.

At the dark moon,
I let go of that
which no longer serves me.

As a quick reference, the new moon occurs once a month and is a great time for setting intentions and beginning anything new that will grow over time. The two-week period between the new moon and the full moon is the time when the moon is 'waxing', or appearing to grow larger. This is also a great time for any positive, growth-focused magic. The full moon is a great time for spells that are about celebration, psychic skills and dreams, or for spells that need a lot of power.

The two-week period after the full moon is known as the waning moon – it is less effective for positive spell-casting. The only spells that should be cast in this time are banishing spells and spells that are connected with setting boundaries. The dark moon, at the end of this two-week period, when the moon isn't visible in the sky at all, is the time to cast spells for ending things that are no longer working or useful.

Tuesday

Bullet journal: herbs and plants

In your magical bullet journal, create artistic themed pages for different plants and their magical uses. You can use paints or colour pens and pencils to depict them, or you can even stick dry leaves and bits of plants into your journal directly. Research how each plant corresponds to the planets, times of day and year, old traditions and what herbal properties they have.

For instance, apples have a magical correspondence to the astrological sign of Taurus, to the faery realm, to the pentagram (if you cut an apple in half width wise, the seeds form a pentagram shape) and the planet Venus. There are also several old folk traditions relating to apples that you can probably think of – apple bobbing, for one!

Garlic, for example, is associated with the astrological sign of Aries and the planet Mars. It's perfect for protection spells (think vampires) and warding off bad energy – and colds!

Wednesday

Bullet journal: tarot readings/cards

In your magical bullet journal, create artistic themed pages for different tarot cards. In the tarot pack there are 78 cards, with 56 of them organised into four suits: Wands (representing the element of fire), Cups (representing the element of water), Pentacles/Coins (representing the element of earth) and Swords (representing the element of air). These are called the Minor Arcana (the 'smaller mysteries', relating more to everyday concerns), numbered from ace to ten, with four 'court' cards per suit. The other 22 cards are the Major Arcana (the 'larger mysteries', which relate more to the deeper psychological or spiritual forces at work in one's life), which begin with The Fool and end with The World.

Draw or photocopy the cards into your journal and list their traditional meanings as well as your interpretations and associations.

Thursday

Bullet journal: recipes

In your magical bullet journal, create artistic themed pages for different magical recipes. These might be foods to make at seasonal festivals – perhaps from a variety of cultures – or witchy-themed foods such as moon-shaped cookies or recipes for different herbal teas or incenses.

Friday

Bullet journal: dreams

In your magical bullet journal, record your dreams on special pages where you might have drawn or designed special 'dreamy' pages. How you do this is totally up to you! Over time, you'll see if recurring themes, images or locations turn up. You could start to map your dream world.

Saturday

'Write your dreams into reality' spell

There are few things more magical than putting pen to paper and allowing your imagination to soar. Start writing the story of the life you want to live, starring you as a character. Don't limit yourself! Include all the things you fantasise about and want to happen.

Sunday

Poetry for catharsis

Express your emotions by writing poetry. It doesn't have to rhyme, just try to get your raw feelings down on the page. How do your emotions taste, sound and smell? Being able to work through your feelings is an essential skill for a witch.

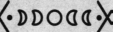

Week 13

Monday

Daily pages ritual

A 'Book of Shadows' is a special book in which witches record their rituals, spell-work, dreams, divination and scrying, as well as other bits and bobs such as recipes for incense or future magical plans.

In your Book of Shadows, write a regular entry (daily, or at least weekly) detailing the moon phase, astrology for the day, your feelings, a note of your dreams and any results or interesting developments from your spell-work. Make a ritual of it to help you concentrate and get connected to your magical inspiration by sitting in front of your altar, lighting a candle and some incense, and centring yourself before you start writing. After you've been doing your daily (or weekly) pages for a while, you'll be able to look back and see your development.

Tuesday

Daily affirmations

Write some of the positive affirmations in this book on bits of paper and put them around your room or in places you will look at them often. Say each affirmation you choose five times daily.

Wednesday

Jade spell for abundance

On your altar, make a little collection of items that represent abundance to you, including a small piece of jade. The items might include some money (the higher the denomination, the better), food, flowers or a pebble from your favourite beach. Hold your hands over the items and feel the power of the earth come through you and into them. Infuse the items with earth power and repeat 'I have abundance and wealth' as many times as you feel is necessary. Keep the jade with you and return it to the altar at night to recharge.

Thursday

Mantra magic!

I am part of nature and nature is part of me

Friday

Writing with nature

Spell out a word with natural foraged finds to represent something you want to manifest into your life. You might use pebbles from a garden, shells from the beach or twigs from the forest. Find somewhere private where you can leave your word for nature to absorb when you've finished.

Saturday

Writing abundance spell

On a day during the two-week waxing-moon period, write a list of all the things that represent abundance to you. Before each item write 'I wish for X'. When you can't think of any more, fold up the paper as small as you can and put it in your purse or wallet.

Sunday

Mantra magic!

I light the fire of creativity in me!

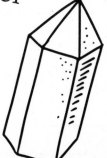

Week 14

Monday

'Writing to your future self' spell

Think about writing letter to your future self and decide when in the future you are writing the letter for. Five years' time? Ten? Write down what you see for yourself in the future and perhaps what your life is like now. Then, put the letter in an envelope, seal it and write your name and the year you want to open it on the front. Keep the letter in a safe place until then!

Tuesday

'Releasing what's over' spell

Light a black candle on your altar. Write down everything that you are ready to release on a piece of paper. Be thankful for the lessons and gifts that these experiences have brought to your life, then burn the paper in a heat-proof dish or cauldron using the candle flame, in a safe manner. If you'd like to, you can also inscribe what you are releasing on to the candle too, before you light it.

Wednesday

Write your own spells

Spell writing isn't difficult, but shorter and simpler is best, and if you can make your short lines rhyme, even better. This makes them easier to repeat and remember. Take a goal or intention and write down what you want to happen, then add a line about achieving this fast, with peace or happiness or for your own highest good. Practise writing spells and compare them to ones in books or online. Don't be afraid to use modern language – spells don't have to sound old-fashioned!

Here's one you can adapt for your own purposes:

I command and direct universal energy to (your goal), with speed, peace and happiness and in accordance with my own highest will and good.
So mote it be!

If you'd like something rhyming, what about:

Blessed be, so mote it be,
Bring my (goal) to me.
Happy be, peaceful be,
Bring it to me
three times three!

Thursday

Mantra magic!

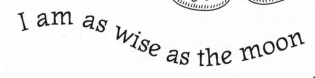

I am as wise as the moon

Friday

Bubble bath ritual for clarity

This is the ritual to perform before an important day, when your wits need to be sharp and your mind as clear as a bell. Add a few drops of cypress or eucalyptus oil to your bath before getting in. Take some deep breaths as you relax and repeat this mantra ten times:

I have clarity; I can think clearly

Saturday

Mindful eating ritual

Take a small food item such as a grape or a strawberry. First, experience what it feels like on your fingers. How does it smell? Press it against your lips. How does it feel? Now, take a bite and really taste it. Can you move it around your mouth and see what different sensations there are? Finally, swallow it and notice how this feels. Practising mindful eating can give you peace of mind and help you stay in the moment.

Sunday

Mantra magic!

Inside me, love; around me, hope; within me, magic!

Week 15

Monday

'Take a breath' ritual

Whenever you need a moment to gather your thoughts and find peace, stop what you are doing (provided it's safe to do so) and concentrate on feeling the sensation of your breath going in and out of your nostrils. Do this as often as you can to restore a sense of centredness and calm.

Tuesday

'Awaken your witch energy' ritual

Connecting to your energy is an important part of magic, and you can awaken your witch energy by practising this technique often.

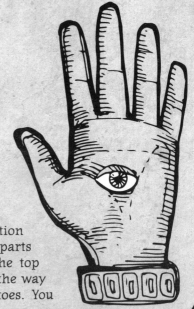

First, move your attention slowly through different parts of your body. Start from the top of your head and move all the way down to the end of your toes. You could focus on feelings of warmth, tension, tingling or relaxation of different parts of your body. Then, when you feel fully present, imagine a ball of light at your belly button. Imagine this ball growing into an egg shape of golden light that surrounds your whole body. Each time you breathe in, imagine the egg growing stronger and more golden. Imagine yourself full of magical energy within this egg, which is nourished by the immense power of the stars. Stay within this magical energy for a few minutes, feeling it radiate through your body, and then open your eyes and make sure you ground yourself by having something to eat or drink.

Wednesday

Music streaming scrying spell

Put one of your music playlists on shuffle and press play. The song that plays will have a message for you – listen carefully to the lyrics and take notice of how the song affects your mood.

Thursday

Mantra magic!

I trust in the universe's plan for me

Friday

Universal love meditation

Lie on your bed and place a small piece of rose quartz where your heart is. Focus on your heart and imagine it as a pink rose opening its petals. As it opens, breathe all the love in the universe into your heart. Imagine the universal love as golden light. Know that there is an unending supply of love available to you. Continue for as long as feels good and keep the piece of rose quartz close to you in a pocket or a bag.

Saturday

Reading uplifting poetry

Research some poets who have written uplifting poems that resonate with you. You could look in the library or online. When you find poets you like, read more of their work and find some favourite poems that fill you with joy.

Sunday

Mantra magic!

I am loved and cherished

Week 16

Monday

Yoga for self-love: cat/cow

An easy, daily pose that introduces flexibility to your back is called cat/cow. Get on your hands and knees with your knees hip-width apart. First, drop your belly and look up: this is cow pose. Then, arch your back like a cat and look down. This is cat pose. Alternate between the two for a while, enjoying the movement it gives to your back. When practising this pose, you can also focus on feeling a line of energy from the top of your head down through your spine. Imagine that every time you take in a breath, you are breathing sun energy into the top of your head. When you breathe out, imagine that you are releasing this energy back to the earth. If you like, as you repeat the cat/cow pose, you can say 'Energy from the sun' in your mind on the in-breath, and 'Energy to the earth' on the out-breath.

Tuesday

Yoga for self-love: figure 4 stretch

To stretch your hips and legs, a supine 'figure 4' stretch is ideal. This is also a lovely pose to practise feeling connected to the earth.

To do the pose, lie on your back. Put both feet on the floor and bend your knees. Now, raise one leg and hug your knee in to your chest, then rest your foot on top of your other knee (look at pictures on the internet if you're not sure how this should look). Now, grab your other leg under the knee with both hands and draw it gently to you. You should feel the stretch in your hips and thighs.

As you do the figure 4 stretch, feel your back melt into the ground and imagine the deep power of the earth fill you with vitality.

Wednesday

Simple meditation for self-love

Lie down comfortably in a calm space where you won't be disturbed. Take some deep breaths with your hands on your heart. On the in breath, think I am worthy; on the out breath, think I am enough. Feel your heart opening, releasing negative feelings. Continue for five to ten minutes.

Thursday

Yoga for self-love: child's pose

An easy pose to do daily, to stretch your back but also to feel calm and centred, is child's pose. On a yoga mat or carpet, kneel with your legs the width of a yoga mat and reach forward with your arms while your bottom goes backwards and down. If you can, rest your forehead on the mat. Take in several deep breaths.

While you are in child's pose, focus on your third eye chakra, which is in the middle of your forehead. The chakras are a series of energy centres in the centre of your body, all of which have different qualities, colours and energies. Feel the sensation of the chakra on the mat, if it's touching it. Imagine the chakra as a deep purplish-blue flower, opening gently as you breathe in and out in the pose. As you relax more and more deeply, repeat 'I am open to my intuition' at least five times while doing this visualisation.

Friday

'Feel your feelings' meditation

Breathe in and out, noticing your breath. Start to focus on your heart as you meditate and notice the emotions you feel. There are no right or wrong feelings here: whatever you feel is valid and needs to be expressed. Give yourself the gift of allowing yourself to feel your feelings for as long as you need to. Repeat regularly.

Saturday

Yoga for self-love: mountain pose

An easy pose to do daily to feel calm and centred is mountain pose. Stand up straight with your hands by your sides, palms facing forward – you can do this anywhere, but in front of your altar will give you a strong sense of focus and power. Stand with your shoulders back and your weight perfectly balanced on both feet. Hold yourself from your core and feel strong. Take in a deep breath in through the nose, and out through the mouth. Repeat this as you focus on your altar and the magical items it holds. Meditate on their symbolism as you stand in the pose.

Sunday

Yoga for self-love: morning stretch

On a yoga mat or carpet, lie down on your back and stretch your arms above your head with your arms by your ears, and point your toes so that your legs are also stretching. If possible, lie either north to south or east to west as you stretch (use the compass app on a phone to show you where the compass points are) and focus on connecting to the two elemental points as you do so (east = air, south = fire, west = water, north = earth).

Enjoy the full-body stretch this gives you. Relax and repeat a few times until you feel energised.

Week 17

Monday

Good luck friends spell

Pick two treats that you both like to eat, one for you and one for your friend. Sit together and think carefully about what you truly want. Then, out loud, take in turns to say out loud what you want to bring into your life. When you have finished, eat your treats together to complete the spell.

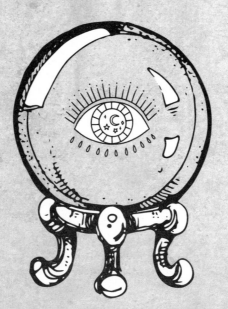

Tuesday

Say goodbye ritual

This is a fun ritual to perform with a group of friends, or coven – a gathering of witches – if you want to shed negative vibes together. Gather up some dried leaves or fallen petals and pile them high in a basket or box. Sit in a circle with the box in the middle – this is best performed outside to avoid a big clean-up operation afterwards! Each person in turn picks up a handful of dried leaves or petals and says what they want to say goodbye to – it could be negative thoughts, bad memories, an aspect of their lives or a person. They then throw the leaves and petals over their left shoulder. Go round the circle until there are no leaves or petals left. Allow the discarded leaves to disperse in the wind and decompose, so that new positive things can flourish in their place.

Wednesday

Texting spell for a friend in need

A text message is a great way to send a friend a little magical boost. If a friend is having a tough time and needs some courage and confidence, find an image of the astrological symbol for Mars, which represents inner-strength and hope, and send it in a text with the words:

Sending you might,
Sending you power,
Sending you strength in
your darkest hour!

Astrological symbol for Mars

Thursday

Mantra magic!

Say to yourself whenever you need to hear it:

I am magic!

Friday

Get in touch spell

If someone has gone incommunicado – difficult to get in touch with – and you want them to message you, get yourself a sticky note, write their name and the date that you would like them to contact you and why on the sticky side. Place the sticky note on your phone screen. Pick out some dried herbs from the kitchen cupboard and sprinkle them over the sticky note. Think about the person for a few moments, then leave your phone to work its magic!

Saturday

Dance grounding-ritual

You can use dance or gentle movement to ground yourself. Listen to some music and dance to it however you want to, but slowly bring your body closer and closer to the ground. End up sitting or lying on the ground and feel it under your body. Feel any negative or nervous energy you need to release sinking into the ground and let it go.

Sunday

Mantra magic!

Positive vibes only!

Week 18

Monday

Fragrant clothes self-love spell

Making your clothes smell nice when you take them from the wardrobe or drawer is a lovely way to lift your mood. Add a few drops of your favourite essential oils to some cotton wool pads, let them dry in a lidded box and then put them among your clothes.

Tuesday

Cake grounding-ritual

A traditional part of a witchcraft ceremony is the grounding phase at the end, once the circle has been opened and the magic performed. This is sometimes called cakes and ale, and as well as being a fun time to chat and relax with your coven, it's a necessary part of the ritual to ground yourself back in the material world and your body. The easiest way to do that is by eating and drinking! For your own cakes and ale ceremony (no ale is needed – fruit juice or water is perfect), eat something healthy and yummy and drink something, too. As you eat and drink, know that it is grounding your body and giving you nutrition and strength.

Wednesday

Time in nature self-love ritual: water

Find a stream or other natural water source. If it's safe
to do so, dip your toes into the water and have a splash!
Allow yourself to enjoy the simple pleasure of the feel of
the water on your skin, its sounds, its appearance and
even its smell. Know that your body is mostly water. Give
love to the water and feel its love for you.

Thursday

Mantra magic!

I am protected by earth, air, fire and water

Friday

Water scrying

This method of fortune-telling is also known as
hydromancy. Use a clear glass mixing bowl or dish and
fill with water. Add a few drops of food colouring to
darken the water and create patterns on the surface –
blue, purple or black is best. Relax your eyes, take some
deep breaths and calm yourself into a meditative state.
See what images appear, or whether you experience
strong feelings or unlock memories in your mind. Be
open to whatever happens and note down your results.

Saturday

Time in nature self-love ritual: fire

Light a candle and stare into the flame. Connect with the spirit of fire – feel its creativity, its heat and unpredictability. Know that you can't live without fire and know that fire represents the life in your body, your active spark and your creativity.

Sunday

Mantra magic!

Kindness surrounds me

Week 19

Monday

Borage salad for self-love

Borage is a common herb you can find in a garden centre or buy online. It's known to stimulate adrenaline and boost mood. You can eat the pretty blue flowers and the leaves (they taste like cucumber), so sprinkle some in your salad for a quick mood boost!

Tuesday

Cooling borage water

Because borage has a cucumber-like taste, you can infuse it in sparkling water with some lemon and perhaps a few strawberries for a delicious drink to help boost self-love. Put some of the pretty blue flowers in too!

Wednesday

Sweet self-love rose cordial

To encourage self-love, make a sweet cordial with 20 dried rose petals, honey and 100ml water. Bring to a simmer in a saucepan and, once cooled, add some sparkling water. Delicious!

Thursday

Mantra magic!

I believe in my infinite potential!

Friday

Morning mood-boost spell

Cinnamon is one of the spices associated with love and brings a delicious warmth and spiciness to food and drink. For a quick mood boost, add a sprinkle of cinnamon to your coffee in the morning, or add cinnamon to a favourite cereal, or even to a milkshake!

Saturday

Porridge spell for self-love

Oats are said to release the soul from sadness. Make a pot of porridge in the usual way but stir the shape of a heart into the mix with a wooden spoon as you do so. Infuse your porridge with love and then eat it.

Sunday

Mantra magic!

I am grateful for all of my gifts

Week 20

Monday

Crystal grid spell

A crystal grid is a magical tool that requires a few crystals symmetrically arranged over a sacred symbol, such as a pentagram or the sacred flower of life, which you can find online.

Set your intention for the grid. What do you want to draw to you? Write your intention and place it under the grid.

Now select crystals that match your intention: rose quartz for love, amethyst for psychic ability or citrine for prosperity. Clear quartz works for everything so feel free to use that if you don't have anything else. Arrange the crystals along the lines of the shape at regular intervals. Now, imagine drawing the shape with your finger in white light over your grid, activating it. Imagine power flowing through you from the earth and from the stars and into your grid. Spend some time each day feeding your grid with positive energy and thoughts. You can take the grid down once your intention has been achieved.

Tuesday

Hematite anti-stress and anti-anxiety spell

On a full moon, light a black candle. Dip your hematite crystal into a small bowl of water (or a cup on your altar). Repeat 'I am safe. I am loved. I am strong and focused.' Allow the crystal to soak in the water under the full moon and focus on it as the candle burns. Then, when you're ready, extinguish your candle and take your crystal and keep it with you as a source of protection and focus.

Wednesday

Ring the changes ritual

Bells are traditionally hung on your door to protect your home. There are all manner of little bells you can source cheaply and hang up. Alternatively, it's handy to have a little bell or a singing bowl – a metal bowl with a wooden striker – that can make a nice ringing sound at the start or end of a spell or ritual. You can also use bells as a way to cleanse your space with sound – just ring them and visualise the room being filled with their good vibrations!

Thursday

Mantra magic!

I am worthy and I am enough

Friday

Stick and paper scrying

Draw a cross on a square of paper or card and write four possible easy answers to a question, one in each square. Ideally, these would be something like GOOD, BAD, NEUTRAL, CHAOTIC or another four outcomes of your choice. Ask your question and drop a small stick onto your paper. Wherever it lands, that's your outcome.

Saturday

Lapis lazuli spell for new friends

Light a pink or green candle and burn some incense. Hold your lapis lazuli to your heart and ask for lovely, kind and fun new friends to come to you. If you can, source a wire cage for your crystal and add it to a necklace so that you can wear it where it's visible, to attract the new friends you will soon meet!

Sunday

Amethyst spell for psychic development

Light a white or purple candle and some incense. Hold your amethyst to your third eye chakra (in the middle of your forehead) and set the intention that it will help open your third eye and improve your psychic ability and dreams. When you feel that you have connected with the crystal, blow out the candle. Leave the amethyst on your altar until you go to bed and put it under your pillow. Sleep with the crystal under your pillow or on your bedside table every night. Note down your dreams.

Week 21

Monday

Witch's ladder spell

A witch's ladder is a traditional knot-tying spell that can be used for anything where there is a specific goal in mind – mental focus for exams, new friends, protection of your home, etc. You should keep some wool handy for this – some witches like to add beads or buttons. If you do, you will need nine, but you can do it just with the wool. Decide on your focus for the spell. Tie three lengths of wool together at the top. Start making a plait. Every few centimetres, add in a knot, or knot in a bead or a button too. Every time you make a knot, concentrate on the outcome of your spell.

Traditionally, the rhyme you say along with the knotting is:

By knot of one,
the spell's begun,

By knot of two,
the magic becomes true.

By knot of three,
so shall it be,

By knot of four,
the power is stored.

By knot of five,
my will shall drive,

By knot of six,
the spell I fix.

By knot of seven,
the future I leaven,

By knot of eight,
my will be fate.

By knot of nine,
what is done is mine.

Tuesday

Rhodonite spell for well-being

Pour a lovely bubble bath and light some candles. Put on some
of your favourite relaxing music. Put the rhodonite crystal in
your bath and draw a pentagram and a heart on the surface
of the water. Let the well-being vibes infuse the water. Get in,
relax and put the crystal on your tummy or your heart. Enjoy!

Wednesday

Fluorite spell for focus

Put the fluorite crystal next to the thing you are trying
to focus on, for example. a book or your laptop. If you're
having trouble concentrating, hold the crystal for a
moment and close your eyes, connecting with its energy.
Then return to your task.

Thursday

Malachite spell for confidence

Wash your malachite in some warm water and dry it. Sit
comfortably and hold the crystal in your hands in your
lap. Imagine the power of the earth rising into you from
beneath you and powering your crystal, and the light
of the moon and stars coming down into you through
the crown of your head and down into the crystal. Now
imagine and feel the power of confidence building in the
crystal and growing around it and you, until it becomes a
sphere of green light around you. Sit with this energy for
a while and feel confident and grounded. When you're
ready, keep the malachite with you and go about your
day but know that the confident aura will stay with you.

Friday

Labradorite spell for wisdom

Take your labradorite with you to the library. Hold it in your hand and ask it to guide you to a book you need to read. Let yourself wander and not think too much about where you go. Take what you're drawn to. There will be wisdom for you there.

Saturday

Rutilated quartz spell for cleansing the aura

Put your crystal in a small bowl of water. Let the crystal infuse the water overnight on a full moon. The next day, transfer the crystal water to a small, clean spray bottle and spritz it all over yourself to cleanse your aura. Spritz daily.

Sunday

Howlite spell for combatting anger

If you are angry, put a piece of howlite in your pocket and go for a run, or dance in your room. Concentrate on expelling as much of your anger energy as you can and feel the howlite helping you.

Week 22

Monday

Sodalite spell for joy

Light a white candle on your altar. Put some music on that gives you a sense of joy. Dance around, holding your sodalite. Pour all your joy into it. Keep the crystal on you in the daytime to keep the joyous vibes going!

Tuesday

Orange calcite spell for happiness

Take your crystal outside under the sun (or in the daylight, if it's winter) and sit with it in your hands, letting it charge in the light. Close your eyes and imagine a sphere of orange energy powering up your crystal and growing all around you. Feel its happy, positive energy. Sit for as long as you like and then go about your day but keep your calcite with you and hold it when you want a burst of pure HAPPINESS!

Wednesday

Clear quartz spell for healing

Lie down on your bed and place your clear quartz over your heart, or, if you have more than one piece of crystal, place them on your forehead, heart and tummy. Relax, take some deep breaths, and close your eyes. Ask the universe for healing and imagine a golden light coming from the crystals, cleansing your aura. Continue for as long as feels good, then place the crystals on your altar and eat a snack and drink a glass of water.

Thursday

Mantra magic!

I am in charge of my life

Friday

Snowflake obsidian spell for balance

If you have a tarot deck, take out the Justice card and place it on your altar. Light a white or blue candle and place your crystal in front of the tarot card. Meditate on the image of Justice and everything it represents about balance. Hold the crystal and feel its energy helping to balance you: physically, emotionally and mentally. Keep the card on your altar as a focus if you like while you seek balance in your life and meditate with your crystal often.

Saturday

Simple crystal charging spell

Wash your crystals in warm water and then leave them in the light of the full moon (on a windowsill is good) to charge them with moon power!

Sunday

Mantra magic!

I am blessed by the moon

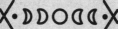

Week 23

Monday

New moon intention-setting ritual

Set up your altar space and draw a circle around you,
ideally using all four elements in turn. Call in all four
elements, starting in the east and working clockwise,
imagining all their power coming into your circle. Light
a white candle and either engrave your intention (one
or two words works best) on to it with a needle, pin or
(carefully!) the end of a knife or a pair of scissors, or
write it on a piece of paper. Focus on the power from
each element infusing the candle and/or the paper. Burn
the paper in the flame and imagine your intention being
released into the world. Write down the steps you can
do to put your intention into action. When you're ready,
close the circle and thank the elements for their help.

Tuesday

Vision board spell

Get a notice board of a decent size or a large piece of
paper or cardboard. Think about what you want to
manifest and find pictures that represent that. You can
use images from magazines, newspapers, printed from
the internet, or you can draw things yourself. Pin or stick

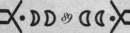

the images to your board – you can also add significant phrases or words, too, if you like. Look at the board every day. Giving the visuals your attention will help manifest those things in your life.

Wednesday

Blackberry crumble for self-love

Blackberries have properties that combat tiredness and overexertion. In summer, find some wild-growing blackberries in hedges and pick a punnet or two (avoid the ones that grow by roads). Stew them with sugar for a delicious dessert or add to stewed apples and make a crunchy, sweet crumble topping for the ultimate comfort food.

Thursday

Mantra magic!

I am beautiful exactly as I am

Friday

Dreamcatcher

A dreamcatcher is a craft belonging to many Native American traditions, and its purpose is to catch bad energies before they get to you, so that you only have good dreams.

You can make your own dreamcatcher with some wool, some cardboard or a plastic ring from a craft shop and some foraged feathers and random beads. Begin by making a ring out of cardboard about an inch thick and about seven inches in diameter. Bind the ring completely in wool by wrapping it over and over, and then (either using a thick needle or your fingers) thread more wool from one side to the other of the ring, making a web. You can find how-to videos online for how to get the signature dreamcatcher look. Now, tie on some feathers or strings of beads so that they're hanging off the bottom of the ring. When you've made it, hang it above your bed.

Saturday

Familiar spell

A familiar is an animal that helps a witch with spells or gives them witchy power. If you have a pet, think of its power as loving you and providing essential cuddle time which makes you chill out and be a better witch! A simple spell here is just to look after your pet – groom it (if it has fur!), get it a new toy or some super healthy food or snacks – and say 'I love you' of course!

Sunday

Mantra magic!

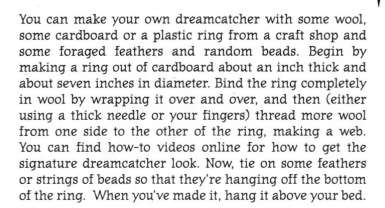

Blessings upon me and blessings upon those around me

Week 24

Monday

Email signature spell

An easy way to add some witchy oomph to your emails (and thus make your communications better received and more effective) is to make your email signature magic.

In your email, find the area where you can adjust your signature and add an image of a powerful symbol of your choice – it might be a combination of runes as a magical sigil, a pentagram, a planetary symbol or another image you love – or perhaps something you've drawn yourself and taken a picture of.

You might also like to add a magic mantra or saying to your email signature – take one that you like from the many in this book! Or, if you'd like to be a little more mysterious, try adding a phrase you like in Latin or another language at the bottom of your emails. Some examples might be:

Pecunia venit ad me

– Money is coming to me

Fortuna, prosperitas et abundantia habeo omnia

– Luck, prosperity and abundance are mine

Amor vincit omnia

– Love conquers all

Tuesday

Jar of wishes spell

On a new moon, write your goals – short term and long term are both fine – on individual pieces of paper and place them into a jar. Put the jar by a window so that your goals can be nurtured by the light of the sun and moon. At the full moon, look at your wishes and see what work you have done towards some of them. At the dark moon, review the goals and take out any that have been achieved. At the next new moon, add more in and continue with the cycle!

Wednesday

Moon-water spell

Put out a saucer to collect some rainwater on the night of a full moon, then transfer it to the cup on your altar, or to a little bottle where you can keep it until you want to use it. You can use this moon-water in a variety of ways: to spray in your space when you are meditating, to use in a ritual or to add to your bath water for some added magic. You can also supercharge your moon-water by adding a moonstone, to give it even more moon energy.

Thursday

Mantra magic!

I am strong.
I am invincible!

Friday

New/waxing moon optimism ritual

Organise and clean your space, including your altar. Ideally, you should clean it and give it a refresh every new moon. Source some bright yellow flowers – daffodils would work well. Put the flowers in a vase somewhere central in your space – or on your altar. Every day until the full moon (you might need to replace them if they don't last the full two weeks!) take a moment to stand in front of your altar and connect to the energy of the flowers – you could even say one or two magic mantras from this book to make the ritual more special. Consciously breathe joy into your heart every time you look at them, as if you could somehow inhale the essence of the flower and its brightness.

Saturday

Animal messages

Different animals represent various qualities in many cultures. If you see an animal that seems out of place, or your attention is drawn to it more than usual, take it as a sign and look up what that animal means. For instance, a toad crossing your path means transformation is coming, and a fox can mean your magic is working. A crow cawing loudly at you may be a reminder for you to pay more attention to your magic – it's OK, everyone gets distracted by real life sometimes – and a deer can be a reminder that we need more gentleness and grace in our lives.

Sunday

Mantra magic!

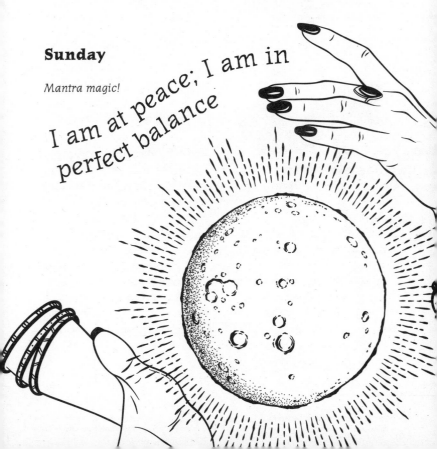

I am at peace; I am in perfect balance

Week 25

Monday

New/waxing moon new love ritual

Light a pink candle and some incense – any will do, but something sweet like rose, ylang-ylang or jasmine would be most effective. Lie down – either on your bed or somewhere calm and beautiful outside, like a meadow. Visualise your heart opening as if it was a pink rose opening its petals, and a new love coming into your life. Feel happy and content that this love is already with you.

Tuesday

New/waxing moon fresh start ritual

The new moon phase is an auspicious time for growth and nurturing hopes and dreams. Find a seed and place it in your hands. Meditate with it and visualise your seed being filled with potential for a wonderful fresh start in whatever way you need. Plant your seed in a pot, water it and place it in sunlight, paying it regular attention. If your altar is in sunlight, that's great, but otherwise a windowsill will do fine.

Wednesday

Simple full moon self-care ritual

Full moons can be intense, so ground yourself with a breathing ritual. Breathe deeply and steadily into your belly, and feel your abdomen go in and out. Repeat the mantra 'I am calm, I am earth' as many times as you need to, remembering that you are made of earth just like all of nature. Repeat this practice every time you feel overwhelmed.

Thursday

Full moon intuition development ritual

Set up your altar – light the candle and put water into the cup or container on your altar. Light some incense – any kind will do. Take a minute to centre yourself and ask that you will receive guidance on how to deepen your intuition from your higher self and the moon during this ritual. Sit and feel yourself connect with earth energy, and then feel the top of your head connect to the light of the full moon. Imagine the moonlight shining around you and within you. Meditate and receive any messages – these might be visions, images, sounds, songs, words – anything that comes is fine. When you feel you're done, thank the moon for its presence, write down your impressions and extinguish your candle and incense.

Friday

Full moon self-love ritual

Run a bath and add some rose oil to the water. Light some candles – white or pink if you have them, but plain tea lights are also fine. You might also like to play some harmonious music you enjoy. If you'd like to, scatter some rose petals into the water. Get in the bath, lie back, close your eyes and make yourself think of five things that are great about yourself. Now, think about one lovely thing you can do for yourself in the next month and plan to do it.

Saturday

Full moon ritual for forgiveness

Centre yourself and take some deep breaths. Feel the light of the full moon shining into your heart and letting you release the hurt you have held there. Cry, laugh or shout and let it all go.

Sunday

Full moon celebration ritual

Invite some friends around for a full moon party! If you can be outside (weather permitting) that would work best. Welcome your friends to the party with a simple ceremony. Ask them to take off their shoes and socks and join you around your altar (you can set this up outside or inside). Light the candle and some incense and draw the circle around you. Call in the elements. Take a moment to ask the full moon for her blessings for all of you. Tell your friends to look up at the moon (if you can see it from where you are) and take a quiet moment to meditate on it. If your friends want to talk about their impressions and feelings, encourage them to do so. Then, dissolve the circle and thank the elements for attending and bid them hail and farewell.

Then, play some upbeat music, dance, eat, drink and be silly – a full moon is a high energy moment to let go and just be.

Week 26

Monday

Simple dark moon self-care ritual

Run a bath. Add in some plain bath salt. Get in and soak. Imagine all your worries being cleansed from you and repeat the mantra 'I am cleansed, I am free and full of light'. When you drain the bath, imagine all your worries draining away with the water.

Tuesday

Dark/waning moon protection ritual

Set up your altar space and draw a circle around you. Call in all four elements in turn, starting in the east and working clockwise, imagining all of their power coming into your circle. In your mind's eye, see the magic circle surround you like a large sphere of white or blue light, above and below ground, so that the sphere encloses you totally. Now, imagine that sphere of light getting bigger so that it grows to include your room and your home. Imagine the sphere to be hard like glass and mirrored, so that it reflects bad energy away from you and your home. When you're ready, close your circle, thanking the elements and know that the sphere of protection remains.

Wednesday

Dark/waning moon banishing bad vibes ritual

Cleanse your space (your house/bedroom) first by cleaning it thoroughly – vacuuming, dusting, tidying! Then, banish bad energy by ringing a bell. Ring the bell in all the corners of the room or in each room, and around each doorway and window. As you do so, say the words 'This is a clean space, I banish all bad energy from this space.' If inside, open a window. Imagine the bad vibes disappearing out of your window.

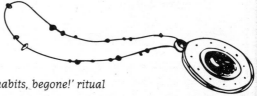

Thursday

Dark/waning moon 'bad habits, begone!' ritual

Light a black candle on your altar. Write down a bad habit you want to banish on a piece of paper. Burn the paper in the candle flame and drop it into a safe receptacle (a cauldron is useful).

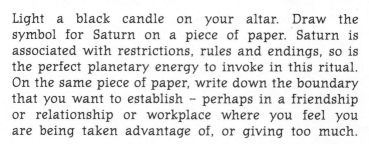

Friday

Dark/waning moon boundary-setting ritual

Light a black candle on your altar. Draw the symbol for Saturn on a piece of paper. Saturn is associated with restrictions, rules and endings, so is the perfect planetary energy to invoke in this ritual. On the same piece of paper, write down the boundary that you want to establish – perhaps in a friendship or relationship or workplace where you feel you are being taken advantage of, or giving too much.

Burn the paper in the flame, asking Saturn to help you build and keep this boundary and create safe space for yourself.

Astrological symbol for Saturn

Saturday

Simple ritual for a solar eclipse

Light a yellow candle. Write I will fulfil my destiny on a piece of paper and burn it in the candle flame. Meditate and be open to the impressions that come to you after having done this. When you feel ready, extinguish the candle.

Sunday

Solar eclipse activity to connect with your destiny

If you know your time, place and date of birth, look up your horoscope online (there are websites that will create a free chart for you) and look at where your Tenth House is. This is the house of your career, legacy and destiny. Solar eclipses can highlight your destiny and provide a sudden glimpse into the future – why not explore it with astrology?

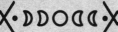

Week 27

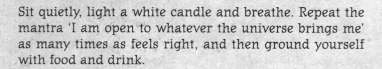

Monday

Simple ritual for a lunar eclipse

Sit quietly, light a white candle and breathe. Repeat the mantra 'I am open to whatever the universe brings me' as many times as feels right, and then ground yourself with food and drink.

Tuesday

Lunar eclipse ritual for self-acceptance

Eclipses can reveal parts of ourselves we may not recognise. Take a bath and meditate in the water by closing your eyes and pay attention to your breath. Now, transfer your attention to your heart and focus on the sensation of breathing in and out while placing your hand on your heart. Now, ask yourself if there is something in your deep self that you could bring into the light and accept? You might have felt ashamed of this part of you before but remember that no part of you is wrong. When you get out of the bath, write your feelings and thoughts in your journal.

Wednesday

Supercharged supermoon ritual

Before you go to sleep, gaze at the moon and then close your eyes and meditate. Go to sleep feeling connected to the moon. You should have some vivid dreams! Note them down when you wake.

Thursday

Mantra magic!

I am blessed by the stars

Friday

Pinterest vision board spell

Create a digital vision board using Pinterest. This can be a mini version of the one you have at home, or a different one for a specific area of your life. For instance, if you are studying for an exam, create a Pinterest board full of helpful images and phrases to help you focus and succeed. Make sure that you look at it often, though, as the key to the effectiveness of vision boards is that you look at them regularly.

Saturday

Thankfulness practice

When we are thankful, it helps us manifest. Every day, say as many thank yous in your mind or out loud for as many things as you can think of. See how it adjusts your energy to a vibration of thankfulness.

Sunday

Dancing manifestation spell

Draw a large circle in your usual way and call in the elements. Have your intention clear in your mind about what you want to manifest. Find an appropriate piece of music (or make a themed playlist!) and dance clockwise around your circle, concentrating on your goal. Imagine the four elements flowing into your circle to help you achieve your goal. Put all the energy you can into your dance, and when you feel the time is right, drop to the ground and earth all that energy, pressing your goal into manifestation into physical reality. Thank the elements and close the circle.

Week 28

Monday

App spell

There is an app for nearly everything these days, so as well as doing spells, see if there's a moon phase app that can help you with your spells. As ever, remember to be safe online, and only use apps that you are old enough to.

Tuesday

Manifesting with plants

If you need a little more money, there are specific house plants that you can grow that have big abundance energy, such as the Chinese money plant or the jade plant. The Chinese money plant is easy to take cuttings from, meaning that in no time you can have a number of lucky money plants. Gift them to friends – the more luck you give out, the more will come your way.

Wednesday ✳ ✳ ✳ ✳ ✳

Make space for the thing you want to manifest

If you have a 'floordrobe', i.e. clothes all over the floor, and items stashed on every surface, and you're not getting the things you truly desire, it might be because there is no room for them in your life. Make room for the things you want, and have a good clear out and tidy, to allow energy to circulate and space to develop for new things. Give old things to charity or re-gift to friends – maybe even have a clothes-swap party. Afterwards, it will be easier for the new things you want to come to you.

Thursday

Mantra magic!

What's meant for me won't pass me by

Friday

Cleaning spell

The number one thing you can do to manifest what you want is to clean out what you don't, and that means dirt. Spring-clean your house or your space. If you want to add some witchy oomph, you can put a sprig of fresh rosemary in a spritz bottle of water and spray it into the corners of your room, saying 'Bad vibes, be gone!'

Saturday

'Say the words' spell

Often, we can want something, but we don't actually speak the words out loud, so it can help to verbalise your desires to a trusted friend. Tell them – and the universe – exactly what you want, and you might find that thing manifests itself. You will be amazed how effective this one simple thing can be.

Sunday

Mantra magic!

I can and I will!

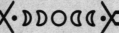

Week 29

Monday

'Do the thing' spell

As well as speaking our desires out loud, it is surprisingly helpful to try to do the thing we want to do. You can start small if it's a big goal, or you might find that with a bit of research and strategic thinking you can achieve the thing you want. Find out how much the thing costs and start a savings plan for it. Or if it's a skill you want to learn, then watch some online tutorials or start a course. Use your bullet journal to create a magic goal page for your particular aim. Write down your research, savings plan or your plan to get what you want and add a magic mantra:

Energy flows where hard work and attention goes

You can repeat the mantra daily, looking at your goal as you have written it in your journal.

Tuesday

Censer for protection

Some witches have a 'censer' on their altar – a wooden or metal container in which you can safely burn loose incense and spells written on paper. The censer is another way to represent the element of air on your altar. A censer is safe to pick up and can be used to draw your circle before a spell for protection.

Wednesday

Midweek optimism spell

If you're feeling a midweek lull and could do with a burst of sunshine energy, a small piece of citrine can help. This sunny yellow stone radiates positive energy and can intensify your manifesting. Place it on your altar, light a yellow candle and meditate on the things that you would like to attract. Speak them into existence as if you already possess these things, for example: I am confident around new people; I attract wonderful new friends and love into my life. Carry the citrine in your pocket or purse as you go about your day.

Thursday

Mantra magic!

Repeat these words at first light:

Today will be a magical day and I will shine!

Friday

Bonfire manifesting spell

If you happen to be near a bonfire, centre yourself by taking some deep breaths and closing your eyes for a moment, feeling the power of the earth flowing up through you from below, and the heat of the fire on your skin. Think of something you want to manifest. Write it on a piece of paper or a leaf and toss it in the flames. Thank the fire spirits for taking your wish. Burning wishes is the quickest way to manifest them!

Saturday

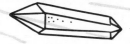

Book of Shadows

This is a special spell book in which you write down all the rituals, procedures, recipes and spells that you have performed. It's also a good place to keep a record of what worked and what didn't, signs you've noticed, scrying outcomes and impressions, tarot questions and answers and dream descriptions. You can stick in pictures like a scrapbook if you like and make a special cover for it.

Sunday

Mantra magic!

I accept what I cannot change

Week 30

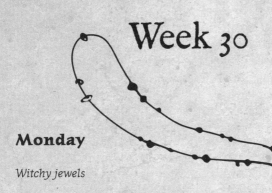

Monday

Witchy jewels

Some people like to wear special
jewellery as a meaningful symbol of
their craft. Pentagram rings or necklaces
are good, but it can be anything that feels
special and witchy to you. After you buy it (or if
it's gifted to you), wash it in clean water then dry
it carefully. Take it to your altar and pass it through
your incense smoke, sprinkle water on it from your cup,
touch it with a crystal or some earth and hold it up to
the candle flame. Ask the moon to cleanse and bless each
new piece of jewellery by bathing it in moonlight (this
should ideally be done around the full moon).

Tuesday

Emoji spell

Since we use symbols so much in spells, why not use
some emojis?

Choose five emojis that are suitable for your desired outcome. For instance, to attract money, you could choose the cash emojis plus a gold star for success and maybe the lightning bolt for speed. For improving your psychic skills, try using the moon in its different phases, the witch and the candle.

When you've made your choices, add the emojis to a text or instant message to yourself and add a relevant mantra, such as MONEY FLOWS TO ME or I AM PSYCHIC, then send to yourself. Repeat daily until your goal has been achieved.

Alternatively, if you have a witchy friend, agree to send your respective emoji spells to each other.

Wednesday

Lovely hashtag spell

As well as only following people you like on social media – unfollow anyone whose content you don't enjoy, life's too short! – you can make your social media experience more '#blessed' by doing a fun little spell with your hashtags. If you think of hashtags like small magical codes, adding positive, powerful hashtags to your posts is another way to attract abundance and positivity to you. You could make up hashtags according to your aims, but word them like positivity mantras. For instance, #IhaveeverythingIneed or #Iammagic or #thankyouformycontinuedblessings are all good. It doesn't matter if the hashtags don't exist, or if they don't have huge numbers of posts. The important thing is that you are making up your own magical codes and putting them into the world.

Thursday

Mantra magic!

I open my heart to all the opportunities that come my way

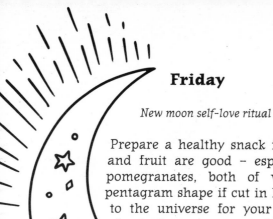

Friday

New moon self-love ritual

Prepare a healthy snack for yourself (nuts and fruit are good – especially apples or pomegranates, both of which show the pentagram shape if cut in half). Give thanks to the universe for your lovely food and know that your personal needs will be met in the month ahead. Toast the new moon with your healthy drink of choice!

Saturday

Online wish list spell

Make an online wish list for everything you want. Trace the shape of a pentagram over the screen with your finger and say 'May I get what I desire'. Send the link to your friends and family!

Sunday

Mantra magic!

I bring magic to the world

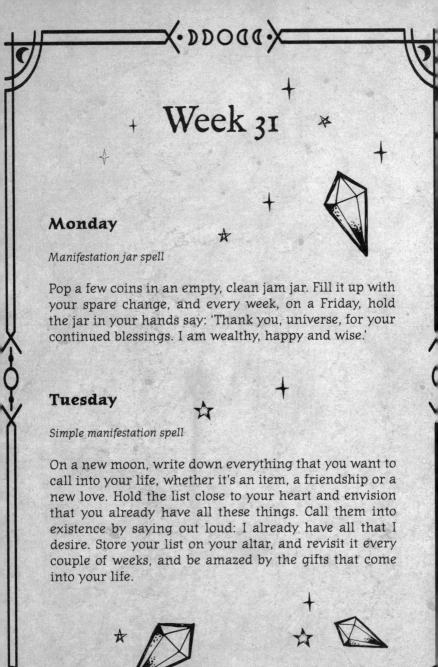

Week 31

Monday

Manifestation jar spell

Pop a few coins in an empty, clean jam jar. Fill it up with your spare change, and every week, on a Friday, hold the jar in your hands say: 'Thank you, universe, for your continued blessings. I am wealthy, happy and wise.'

Tuesday

Simple manifestation spell

On a new moon, write down everything that you want to call into your life, whether it's an item, a friendship or a new love. Hold the list close to your heart and envision that you already have all these things. Call them into existence by saying out loud: I already have all that I desire. Store your list on your altar, and revisit it every couple of weeks, and be amazed by the gifts that come into your life.

Wednesday

Sparkler wish spell

On a clear night, use a sparkler (carefully following the instructions on the packet!) and write what you want in the air with the tip of the lit sparkler. Ask the powers of fire to take your wish and make it a reality.

Thursday

Mantra magic!

I follow my own star

Friday

369 spell

Write down your wish three times as soon as you wake up in the morning, six times in the afternoon and nine times before you go to bed. The number of times you write down your wish represents a way to intensify the focus on manifesting what you desire, and three is a number traditionally associated with the moon because of her triple aspect of waxing, full and waning phases. Ideally, begin on the new moon and repeat the spell every day until the full moon.

Saturday

Star palm magic

If you have little lines on your palms that intersect to look like stars, you are in luck because they are seen as particularly auspicious. If you have a small star shape of crossed lines on your Mount of Luna (at the bottom of your palm opposite your thumb) it means you are very smart and probably artistic. If you have a star on the Mount of Jupiter (below the index finger) it means you will be wealthy, successful and be happy.

Sunday

Mantra magic!

I am good enough

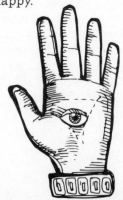

Week 32

Monday

Pendulum spell

Hold a quartz crystal on a chain so that it hangs above the palm of your non-dominant hand. Connect to your intuition and ask the pendulum to show you 'yes'. Hopefully it will show you a movement which will be either swinging in a circle or an oval, or swinging back and forward, or staying still. Make a mental note of what 'yes' looks like. Then ask the pendulum to show you 'no' and make a note of the result. Finally, ask it to show you 'naybe' and note what it does. Now you're ready to ask your questions! Still the pendulum every time before asking a new question – and remember you can only ask yes, no or maybe questions.

Tuesday

Using a pendulum to find lost objects

A pendulum can be a useful tool for when you have lost or mislaid something, but you will need to be creative with your questions as it can only answer with yes or no. Or, if it's something small like a piece of jewellery and you have a vague idea of where it might be, you can hold the pendulum above a piece of furniture or a general location and ask the pendulum if it is there.

Wednesday

'Sweep away bad vibes' spell

After an argument or an upset, the negative vibes can linger and take a while to disperse, leaving you and those around you feeling flat for quite a long time afterwards. To sweep away the bad energy, you're going to need a broom! As you sweep, the negative energy will cling to the dust, then chant:

Swish, swish, out you go, only let the good vibes flow.

Thursday

Mantra magic!

I am afraid of nothing

Friday

Salt cleanse ritual

If you're going to a place that carries bad feelings for you, such as a classroom or a workspace, take a small amount of salt with you and sprinkle it in the four corners of the room – this will cast a safe space for you and clear away the negativity that has settled there.

Saturday

Coffee shop spell

This is a lovely simple spell to perform when you're out and about and you're keen to attract good vibes and unravel bad ones. For good vibes, stir your coffee in a clockwise motion and think carefully about the things that you wish to attract that day. To shake off bad vibes that you are experiencing, stir your coffee 'widdershins' – anticlockwise – and imagine the negativity dispersing and dissolving to nothing.

Sunday

Mantra Magic!

I am worthy of love and happiness

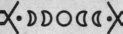

Week 33

Monday

Truth enchantment spell

If you feel that someone is not being truthful to you, try this spell and see what is revealed. You will need a lapis lazuli stone, some salt and a candle for your altar. First, cast a safe circle with your wand or your index finger, light the candle and meditate on the flame. Hold the stone, sprinkle a pinch of salt on it and say the following words:

Remove the false,
Reveal the true,
In all I see,
So mote it be!

Blow out the candle. The stone is now enchanted and will help you to see through lies and dishonesty.

Tuesday

A self-love rose quartz ritual

Life is so much richer and happier when we love and accept ourselves. But self-love needs to be nurtured and cultivated in order to flourish. Perform this simple ritual every night for a week: Hold a small piece of rose quartz in your palm, think about the day and pinpoint three things that you did that you are happy about, and say those things out loud. The stone will become charged with positive self-love vibes and only grow more powerful each time you tell it the things that you love about yourself.

Wednesday

'Make a new friend' spell

If you're feeling lonely and in need of friendship, pick some bay leaves from a bush – or use dried leaves if you have those. Write down some characteristics of the kind of friend you would like, such as funny, kind, outgoing, bookish, on to the leaves with a pen. Then, on a blustery day, throw them out of your bedroom window. You will soon see some like-minded friends entering your life.

Thursday

Mantra magic!

I embrace my destiny

Friday

An exam luck spell

This spell will sprinkle a little bit of luck on you for your big day. Light a green candle on your altar, hold something in your hand that represents the test that you will be taking, such as a paintbrush for an art exam, a calculator for a maths exam. Now say the words:

Luck be with me for my test,
May I always do my best!

Watch the candle flame for a few minutes and visualise yourself acing your exam, now blow out the candle and the spell is cast.

Saturday

Socials spring clean ritual

Sometimes it's good to have a digital clear-out and remove all the associations that no longer serve you. Take some time to go through your connections on TikTok, Instagram, WhatsApp, etc. As you check out of a group chat, or unfollow an account, thank it for the support or purpose it provided and let it go!

Sunday

Mantra magic!

Today will be a magical day

Week 34

Monday

Happy thoughts spell

This spell is for when you might be feeling low or anxious, as it will awaken happy memories and give you a lift. Gather a couple of sprigs of rosemary. Rub the needles between your fingers to release its aroma and say: May rosemary and sunshine, bring happiness that's true and mine.

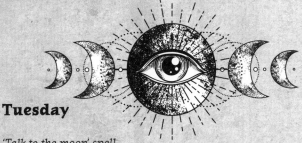

Tuesday

'Talk to the moon' spell

The moon always listens to our thoughts, hopes and dreams, and no more so than when the moon is full. Write down a list of things that you wish to manifest by the next full moon. Find a small silver object that you can keep with you, such as a pendant or ring, and on a full moon night, place it outside to catch the moon's rays to charge it, with your list folded underneath. For the next month, you must keep the piece of silver with you to manifest your desires.

Wednesday

Simple rune reading

Runes are small, flat counters or pebbles with inscriptions which are based on the Futhark alphabet – a writing system used by Germanic peoples and Scandinavians over a thousand years ago. You can make your own by collecting small, smooth stones and drawing the rune symbols on them with permanent markers or making them out of air-drying clay and scoring the letters into the clay with a needle: you can find the shapes and their meanings easily online. When you have your rune set, ask the runes a question and pick one up to find the answer. You can ask questions such as 'What approach should I take to this situation?' or 'What will the outcome be to this issue?' or 'How can I best concentrate on self-care in this situation?'

Thursday

Mantra magic!

I am the author of my own destiny

Friday

Friendship rune reading

Think about a friend and your current situation with them. Draw a rune to represent you in

the relationship, a rune for how your friend is feeling and a third rune for how to progress in your friendship together. For instance, if you drew the rune Sōwilō to represent your attitude in the relationship, Sōwilō means sun and positivity, so it would mean that you have a sunny disposition and outlook toward the other person. If you drew Perth (unclear/lack of clarity) for how your friend was feeling, it would perhaps suggest that they felt a little unsure of the relationship. However, if you drew Wunjō (joy) for how to act in your friendship going forward, the best advice would be to continue being positive to reassure your friend, and you could look forward to joyful times together as a result.

Sōwilō rune symbol

Saturday

Well-being rune reading

Sit with your runes while meditating. When you feel ready, draw one rune, asking to be drawn to the best advice for improving your life right now. Try to focus on a particular aspect of your life to receive the most accurate guidance.

Sunday

Mantra magic!

Today is a gift

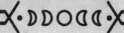

Week 35

Monday

Þ

Rune yoga

Experiment with standing in the positions of the Futhark runes with your legs and arms mimicking their shapes. When you make the shape of the rune with your body, say the name out loud. Practice this like a kind of meditative yoga.

Tuesday

Magical sigil spell

As well as using runes singly, it is possible to make a magical 'sigil' by combining more than one rune into one symbol. You can do this by identifying an outcome, selecting two or three runes that are appropriate for that outcome and drawing a symbol on paper that combines all the lines of all the individual runes into one. This means that there will be some sections that are common to all of the runes and some lines that just come from one.

Sketch out the sigil in your bullet journal or your Book of Shadows until you have the shape of it right, and then make a final version of it in black pen. Now, burn it (safely) and trust that the universe has heard your request and will answer it soon.

Wednesday

Make room in your personal life for the person you want to manifest

To make room for the new people you would like in your life, communicate your clear boundaries in toxic relationships, whether that's with your friends or romantic partners. As well as being clear with the people in your life by talking to them clearly about your needs, likes and dislikes, you can cast a spell on yourself to make sure that you attract someone better for you.

First, on the dark moon, have a salt bath and meditate on all the things you have found toxic in your relationships. Consider what you could have done differently and take responsibility for any part you may have played in any drama, then forgive yourself and know you will do better next time. Release the toxicity you have been holding about this relationship into the water and, when you're ready, drain the bath and visualise the negativity draining away.

The next day, on the new moon, stand in front of your altar. Light the candle and the incense. With a pen and paper, write down all the qualities you would like to attract in a new friend or romantic partner. Read these things out loud, beginning with, 'Dear Moon, please bring me a new friend/boyfriend/girlfriend who is ...' and then ending with, 'All this or something better, in accordance with my own highest will and good.'

Keep the piece of paper under a quartz or other crystal on your altar or under your pentacle.

Thursday

Mantra magic!

I deserve all the good in my life

Friday

Vision board tarot spell

Take one or two tarot cards (or cards from an oracle deck, if you prefer) that really appeal to you in some way. Find cards that represent something you want to manifest in your life, for example, Ten of Cups for a happy family life or Six of Wands for acclaim and fame! Pin them to a vision board and look at them every day. Watch as they make themselves known in your life.

Saturday

Nature-offering ritual

If you are drawn to a certain place, such as a favourite tree, a hill or a stream, for example, make a regular safe and non-toxic offering at your special place, honouring it and thanking it for its beauty and energy. Offerings could be things like a beautiful leaf, a feather, a piece of fruit, or you could even pour some water into the ground. By making regular offerings to nature, you strengthen your connection to the elements and start to build a relationship with that special place, which can become somewhere that you regularly perform magic.

Sunday

Mantra magic!

I have a beautiful life

Week 36

Monday

Moon candle spell for peace

 Carve a crescent moon into a white candle with a pin. Also carve the word 'PEACE' into the side. Burn it and say, 'Beautiful Moon, please give me peace.'

Tuesday

Mars candle spell for energy

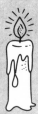 Carve the astrological symbol for Mars into a red candle with a pin. (See page XX for Mars' astrological symbol.) Also carve the word 'ENERGY' into the side. Burn it and say, 'Strong, virile Mars, please bring me energy.'

Wednesday

Mercury candle spell for focus

Carve the astrological symbol for Mercury into an orange candle with a pin. Also carve the word 'FOCUS' into the side. Burn it and say, 'Clever, resourceful Mercury, please give me focus.'

Thursday

Jupiter candle spell for luck

Carve the astrological symbol for Jupiter into a blue candle with a a pin. Also carve the word 'LUCK' into the side. Burn it and say, 'Bounteous, generous Jupiter, please bring me luck.'

Friday

Venus candle spell for self-love

Carve the astrological symbol for Venus into a pink candle with a pin. Also carve the words 'LOVE MYSELF' into the side. Burn it and say, '"Beautiful loving Venus, please help me to love myself.'

Saturday

Saturn candle spell for protection

Carve the astrological symbol for Saturn into a black candle with a pin. Also carve the words 'PROTECT ME' into the side. Burn it and say, 'Stern, strong Saturn, please protect me.'

Sunday

Mantra magic!

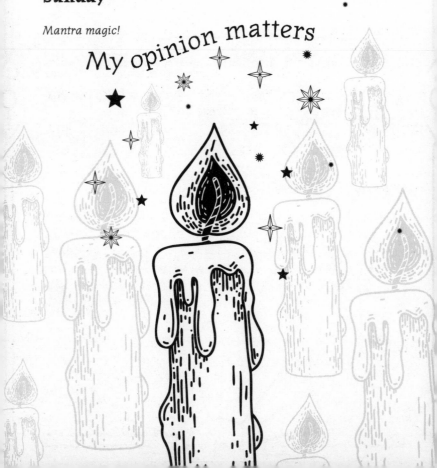

My opinion matters

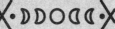

Week 37

Monday

Sun candle spell for happiness

Carve the astrological symbol for the Sun into a yellow candle with a pin. Also carve the word 'HAPPINESS' into the side. Burn it and say, 'Bright, positive Sun, please bring me happiness.'

Tuesday

Goddess candle spell

For this spell you will need a simple candle-making kit, which can be purchased cheaply online. Take a walk in one of your favourite places in nature – the place that you go to feel revived and at peace. Pick up seaweed, small shells, seed pods or dried leaves – small items that will not have an impact on the environment – and take them home. Make the candle according to the instructions in the kit. When the wax is in liquid form, drop in your finds from your special place into the wax. Leave your goddess candle to set. You now have a very special candle filled with happy memories to light for those times when you need a lift.

Wednesday

'I feel beautiful' candle spell

When the moon is waxing – not waning - carve 'I FEEL BEAUTIFUL' into a pink candle, as well as the astrological symbol for Venus. Create an altar space with some roses, a picture of the goddess Venus (also known as Aphrodite – you can find plenty online and print one out in colour) and some sweet-smelling incense. If you have some rose quartz crystals, add those too. You could play some gentle music too if you like or read poetry. Light the candle and the incense and thank the universe for all the gifts of beauty and abundance it has already given you, and ask the universe to make you feel beautiful, lovely, sensual and cherished. Repeat for nine nights, ideally ending on a full moon.

Thursday

Mantra magic!

I radiate inner harmony

Friday

Relaxation bath self-love candle ritual

If you can, source some floating candles, run a bath, adding some rose or patchouli bath oil (or some other nice scent you like) and place the candles on the top of the water. Draw a pentagram in the water with your finger, imagining the star lighting up your bath water with power. Get in the water and light each candle in turn. Every time you light a candle, you will say something nice about yourself, like 'I am kind', 'I am loved', or 'I am a good friend'. Lie back and enjoy the warm water and the scent of the oils. When you're ready, blow out the candles and feel good about yourself.

Saturday

Rosemary candle spell for protection

Anoint a black candle in olive oil and roll it in some dried Rosemary. Burn the candle in a flame-proof container and imagine its energy casting a protective black cloak around you.

Sunday

Mantra magic!

I love my body and all its magic

Monday

Sage candle spell for purification

Anoint a white candle in olive oil and roll it in some dried Sage. Burn the candle in a flame-proof container and imagine its energy casting a protective cloak of purity around you.

Tuesday

Cinnamon candle spell for luck

Anoint a white candle in olive oil and roll it in some powdered cinnamon. Burn the candle in a flame proof container and ask the universe for luck – either generally or in a particular matter.

Wednesday

Mint candle spell for calm

Anoint a white or green candle in olive oil and roll it in some dried mint. Burn the candle in a flame-proof container and imagine it radiating calm in your space and making you calm and focused.

Thursday

Mantra magic!

I protect my joy

Friday

Ginger candle spell for success

Anoint a white candle in olive oil and roll it in some powdered ginger. Burn the candle in a flame-proof container and imagine it radiating an energy of success, either generally or for something specific.

Saturday

'Recovery after a break-up' candle spell

Rub neroli, lavender and rosemary essential oils on to an orange candle. Hold the candle and visualise yourself walking away from the person in question and all the ties between you melting into thin air. Now, burn the candle and let the scents of the oils fill you with new positivity and healing.

Sunday

Mantra magic!

I love myself unapologetically

Week 39

Monday

Better health candle spell

Rub clary sage and chamomile essential oils on to a green candle. You could also carve 'I AM HEALTHY' on to it if you choose. Burn the candle, repeating, 'I am healthy; I have healthy habits.'

Tuesday

Friendship candle spell

To bring good new friends to you or to strengthen the friendships you already have, rub bergamot and geranium essential oils on to a pink candle. Hold the candle, imagining yourself having a great time with your friends. Now, burn the candle and let the scents of the oils fill you with a sense of love for your current friends or the ones you are about to attract to you.

Wednesday

Confidence candle spell

Rub ylang-ylang oil on to a yellow candle and carve I AM CONFIDENT onto it. Light it and imagine the heat from the candle filling you up with confidence and power.

Thursday

Mantra magic!

I am letting go of the things that make me unhappy

Friday

Greater prosperity candle spell

Rub clove, myrrh and olive oil into a green or blue candle. Imagine what prosperity looks like to you as you dress the candle. Is it raining money? Is it having beautiful clothes or a new job, perhaps? Light the candle and make a list of all the things that already make you prosperous and say thank you out loud for each one. Repeat every day for eight days.

Saturday

Home beautiful candle spell

Rub rose, orange blossom and myrrh onto a green or pink candle, imagining beauty and calm radiating from the candle when you burn it somewhere central in your home or your room.

Sunday

Mantra magic!

Good witch energy surrounds me

Week 40

Monday

Self-love spritz spell

Make up a lovely perfume for yourself you can spray in your space, on your sheets, on your clothes and your body any time you want to feel special. Combine three teaspoons of spring water with five drops of rose oil, five drops of rose geranium oil and five drops bergamot oil. Put into a little spray bottle and shake well, then spray!

Tuesday

Mindfulness drawing ritual

Get some pens and paper and start drawing. Don't feel like you have to draw something in particular, just focus on the colours and shapes or the feeling of drawing itself. See if you can lose yourself in the act of drawing or do the same with a colouring book.

Wednesday

Bubble bath ritual for energy

Put a few drops of spearmint, peppermint or rosemary oil in your bath (or a bit of each!) before getting in. Take some deep breaths as you relax and repeat the mantra: I have energy; I am energetic, ten times.

Thursday

Mantra magic!

I love myself completely

Friday

Love letter to yourself spell

Write a letter to yourself as you would to someone you had a crush on – if you were being completely brave and honest about your feelings. Write everything that you love about yourself: all the adorable traits, the nicest parts of you, the loveable things. Then, write about how you also love all the difficult things and the imperfections. Now, seal this letter in an envelope and write your name on the front. Open in one year.

Saturday

Writing about tarot

Starting with The Fool and making your way to The World, focus on using each Major card in the tarot (also called the Trumps) as an inspiration for writing. Take out the card in question and imagine your way into it. What ideas does it spark in you? Write down whatever insight comes.

Sunday

Mantra magic!

I will manifest my desires!

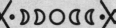

Week 41

Monday

Burning letters spell

Write a letter to someone who has hurt you. Say everything you want to say in the letter: don't hold back. Then, burn it safely or cast it into the sea and know that you have said what you needed to.

Tuesday

Daily gratitude list

Every day, write a list of at least ten things you are grateful for, from your shower to your best friend to your toes, etc. It doesn't matter if you repeat some but try to add in new ones too.

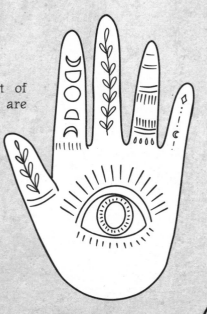

Wednesday

Healthy snack spell

When you are eating your healthy snack, say a mental thank you to the universe for its bounty. Break off a tiny piece of your snack and lay it somewhere that feels meaningful outside as an offering of thanks to nature.

Thursday

Mantra magic!

I give thanks for the abundance in my life

Friday

'One ruler to rule them all' spell

At a pinch, you can use your ruler as a magic wand if you don't have your real wand to hand. Give it a quick clean under the tap and draw a pentagram on it in water with your finger, asking for the blessings of the moon to consecrate your ruler temporarily as a wand. Now, use it for drawing a circle if you like, or for directing energy in a spell if you think you need it.

Saturday

Phone protection spell

An easy and fun way to protect your phone with magic is to set an image of a pentagram (or other protective symbol of your choice) as your phone lock screen, background (or both!). As you do so, trace the pentagram over your screen lightly with your finger and say: 'Air, earth, water, fire, spirit, protect my phone. So be it!'

Sunday

Mantra magic!

I will always believe in myself

Week 42

Monday

Cloud divination spell

Watch the clouds and let your mind be open and clear. Ask the clouds to give you an answer to a question you might have and be open to the shapes that present themselves.

Tuesday

Nature spirit meditation

When you are in nature, such as a forest, a beach, woodland, by a lake, etc., sit quietly, close your eyes and set the intention that you will be at peace with the spirits of that place.

Wednesday

'I am magic' visualisation

Close your eyes and take some centring breaths. Now, visualise yourself as your most magical self. However this looks is up to you, but you could imagine yourself wearing a certain type of outfit, for instance. It doesn't matter what you imagine, as you just need to feel that you are seeing your true, magic, inner self. Visualise yourself as vividly as possible and say to yourself I am magic, exactly as I am.

Thursday

Mantra magic!

My heart is open and kind

Friday

Time in nature self-love ritual: air

Go to a high point in the landscape, such as a hill or cliffs, standing a good distance from the edge. Face the wind or the breeze and feel it on your body, breathe it in, feel its strength and swiftness and also how it changes. Know that oxygen keeps you alive and is part of you. Give love to the air and feel its love in your lungs.

Saturday

Tree root grounding meditation

Stand with your feet firmly on the ground and with your hands by your sides. Close your eyes and imagine roots growing from your feet and burrowing down deep into the earth, grounding you. Know that you are as strong as a tree.

Sunday

Mantra magic!

I forgive myself

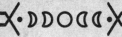

Week 43

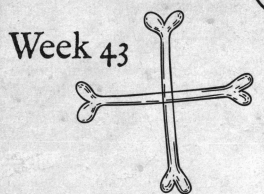

Monday

Four elements ritual

Stand in the middle of your circle, facing east. Call the powers of air and imagine a light breeze spiralling into the centre of your circle. Turn to face south and call the powers of fire. Imagine a line of fire spiralling into the circle from the south. Turn to face west and call to the powers of water. Imagine water spiralling into the circle. Turn to face north and call to the powers of earth. Imagine earth joining the spiral or elements in the centre of the circle. Now hold out your hands and visualise all four elements combined in a moving spiral in your palms. Direct your elemental power to a chosen purpose or wish and imagine that combined elemental power flowing towards your goal. When you are done, thank the elements and bid them farewell.

Tuesday

Forest walk spell

Take a walk in woodland. Feel the ancient power of the trees, earth and plants flowing into you from your feet upwards. Breathe in the wisdom of the forest.

Wednesday

Simple shell wish spell

Find a shell you like, hold it in your hand and define very clearly what it is you want to wish for. Then, throw it into the sea and make your wish.

Thursday

Mantra magic!

I let go of yesterday – today is a fresh start

Friday

Slightly more complicated shell wish spell

On a beach, find a spot where you can see the tideline. If you have a wish in mind, create symbolic pictures of what you want on the sand with whatever is available: shells, grasses, stones, etc. (Don't use trash, though – bin that!) Be mindful and focused with your images. Then, form a circle of stones, shells or materials around your picture and concentrate vividly on what it represents to you. When you feel happy with what you've done, either wait for the sea to come in and take your wishes or leave your offering and know that the sea will take it in its own time.

Saturday

Pebble spell

Find a flat pebble and write the thing that you would like to be free of onto it with chalk, then cast it into the sea.

Sunday

Mantra magic!

I am the change I want to see *

Week 44

Monday

Heart meditation for self-love

Take some deep breaths and breathe into your heart. Visualise love pouring out of your hands and into your heart. Let this love energy collect in your heart and then fill your body. Feel warm and at peace. Know that love is always available for you when you need it.

Tuesday

Social media feed scrying spell

Using whichever social media platform you prefer, focus your mind on a question and then refresh your feed. The post that pops up first has an answer or message for you.

Wednesday

Melted wax scrying spell

Focus on a question or just let your mind open. Carefully pour melted wax from a lit candle onto a dish of water or onto a piece of card. Gaze at the wax and see what images spring to mind.

Thursday

Mantra magic!

I will find a way

Friday

Smoke scrying spell

Light some stick incense in a holder. Gaze into the smoke and watch patterns form in it. Whatever you see, write down in quick notes with a pen and piece of paper – it can be just brief words and phrases. Don't worry about getting it wrong – there are no right or wrong answers.

Saturday

Time in nature self-love ritual: earth

Find a place of natural beauty near to you – it might be a park or a field or a beach, wherever is quiet and beautiful to you. Sit somewhere peaceful and close your eyes. Connect to the earth, allow yourself to feel it, smell it and connect with it as deeply as possible. Know that your body is made of the same stuff as the ground you sit on. Give love to the earth and feel its love for you.

Sunday

Mantra magic!

Every day I am stronger

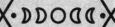

Week 45

Monday

'Tiger's Eye' new beginning spell

Light a yellow candle. Hold a tiger's eye gemstone near your heart, close your eyes and visualise your new beginning. Then repeat: 'I have everything I need. I am excited about my new beginning' five times. Sit with your crystal until you feel it has been charged with the spell energy. Keep the crystal with you until you have achieved your goal.

Tuesday

Rose quartz open-heartedness spell

Hold the rose quartz up to your heart. Set an intention to connect to your feelings and open your heart more. Now, carry the crystal with you and hold it to your heart often, feeling its beautiful energy opening you up.

Wednesday

Feather scrying spell

Feathers can be seen as signs that your spells are working, or messages from the universe that you're not alone. If you find one in an unusual place, take it as a sign!

Thursday

Mantra magic!

I am free from worries

Friday

Candle flame scrying spell

Light a candle, ideally in a dark and quiet room. Stare into the flame and let yourself relax. What images or impressions come to you?

Saturday

Swimming ritual

If you can swim and you have access to an outdoor pool, swim out and float on your back. Lie back in the water (if you can) or, if you can't swim, just stand in the water at whatever level is comfortable. First, thank the water for supporting you, for being always present in your life to nourish and care for you. Then, commune with the element of water. Feel it on your body, but also try to connect emotionally to it. What do you feel? Ask the water for its blessing and offer it your love. The act of being thankful is a powerful magic, as thankfulness and love are emotions that raise our personal vibration and make it easier for us to manifest what we want.

Sunday

Mantra magic!

I trust in myself

Week 46

Monday

Beach meditation ritual

Beaches are special places that hold all four elements in the same place, so are perfect for magic. Stand in the water and commune with all four elements at once, feeling them around you and breathing them in and out. Give your love and thanks to the sea, the air, the ground under your feet and the heat of the sun. Feel that you are perfectly poised at the centre of the elements, and a creature of all of them in equal measure. When you are done, give thanks to all four elements for existing in perfect harmony.

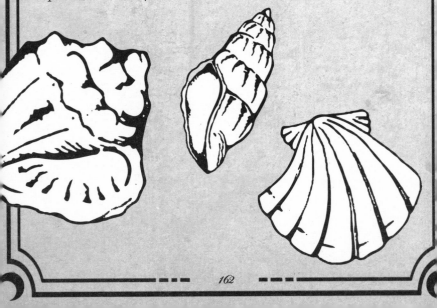

Tuesday

Jasper spell for calm

Turn off your phone, make sure you're alone and sit quietly. Light a scented candle or play some gentle instrumental music. Hold your jasper stone to your throat and breathe in and out deeply. Imagine you are breathing in calm, breathing out worries. Keep the jasper with you and hold it in your hand when you need to feel calm.

Wednesday

Cauldron

A cauldron has many uses, whether you find a full-size one (many cheap, second-hand copper ones can be found online) or a mini one, which are also readily available. Use a full-size one as a safe place to burn your candle spells or fill your cauldron with herbal spells. Mini ones are good on your altar to represent the element of water, or good receptacles for spell bags, hag stones and other witchy ephemera.

When I let go, I grow

Thursday

Mantra magic!

Friday

'Stirring luck' wooden spoon spell

Using a wooden spoon, stir whatever you are cooking in a pan clockwise. Say the following to bless your food and give it extra goodness: Blessed be the earth that grew this food. May we be nourished by it.

Saturday

Quick protection salt spell

Take kitchen salt and either walk around the outside of your property with it, making a large protective circle, or if you can't walk the perimeter of your home, put a line of salt outside your front door to keep negativity away.

Sunday

Mantra magic!

I give myself space to grow

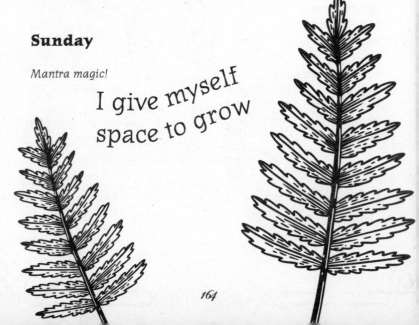

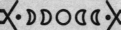

Week 47

Monday

Quick coffee blessing spell

Stir your tea or coffee with a teaspoon and draw the shape of a pentagram on the top of the drink to empower it before you drink it. Drink, and feel just a little more witchy than you did before!

Tuesday

Jam jar candle spell

If you have some old jam jars, clean them, drop in a tea light candle and draw a pentagram or other witchy symbol on the front (permanent marker will do)to make an easy spell lamp.

Wednesday

Kitchen foil freezer spell

If you want someone to leave you alone, write their name on a piece of paper, wrap it in foil and put it in the freezer. That's all there is to it!

Thursday

Mantra magic!

I know my true worth

Friday

Ribbon wishes spell

If you have some odd lengths of ribbon, tie them to a tree and make a wish as you do so. Choose a tree of a good age, in a woodland, forest or park – not one in someone's garden, unless it's yours!

Saturday

Plaiting string good vibes spell

If you have some kitchen string or a ball of wool, you can use it to make a plaiting spell. Tie three lengths of wool or string together at the top and set the intention that you are sending good energy to a friend. As you plait, repeat 'sending love to ...' and then their name. When you get to the end, tie it up and give it to them.

Sunday

Mantra magic!

When my world is dark, I will look for stars

Week 48

Monday

Seasonal foraged wreaths

You can incorporate anything from conkers, leaves, flowers and even fruit, such as apples, into a wreath with some wire and string. Pierce soft conkers with a knitting needle to make a hole in them or gather seasonal leaves and grasses.

Tuesday

Food container spell

Containers such as empty yoghurt pots, jam jars and plastic takeaway cartons with lids are ideal receptacles to be reused for witchy storage. Rather than throw these away, clean them out, make some witchy labels for them and use them to store drying herbs for teas, incense and spells.

Wednesday

Feather fan spell

When you're out and about, collect five or six feathers and bring them home. Glue them together (you'll need a strong glue) at the bases to make a feather fan you can use to waft incense when you're smudging a room.

Thursday

Mantra magic!

I bring serenity to everything I do

Friday

Rowan berry protection bracelet

If you find a rowan tree, collect an odd number of its red berries and use a needle to string them on to a length of red thread. Hang the string somewhere dark and dry until the berries dry out. When dry, tie the ends together to make a bracelet for protection.

Saturday

'Sweet dreams' charm bag spell

Find some scraps of material or cut up an old tea-towel or T-shirt. Make two matching heart shapes at least five or six inches tall and wide and sew them together, leaving a good-sized gap in your stitches. Now, turn the heart inside out and fill with dried lavender and rose petals and stitch up the gap. Add a loop of plaited wool and hang by your bed to promote good dreams.

Sunday

Mantra magic!

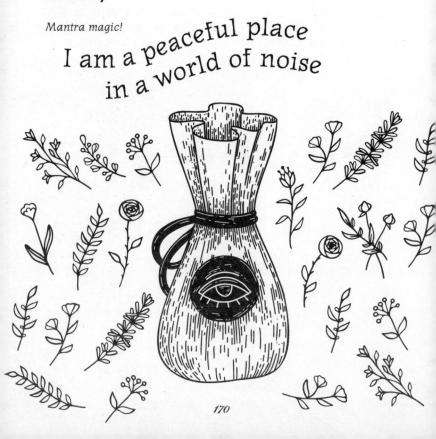

I am a peaceful place in a world of noise

Week 49

Monday

'Hello, Mr Magpie' charm

If you see a lone magpie, remember to salute it and say, 'Hello, Mr Magpie, how's your wife?' Magpies are lucky, but it's considered unlucky to see one on its own. The old rhyme will tell you what the omen is, depending on how many you see:

One for sorrow,
      two for joy,
Three for a girl,
      four for a boy.
Five for silver,
      six for gold,
Seven for a
   secret never
to be told.

Tuesday

Dust be gone spell

Dust away negativity with your duster and a little polish. Clean your room (or the whole house!) wiping away dust and polishing the clean surfaces, saying, 'Negativity be gone! This is a clean room!' Make sure to open a door or window so that negative energy can escape. When done, burn a scented candle or some incense to fill the space with good vibes.

Wednesday

Scissor star spell

Use scissors to cut out a pentagram from paper and add it to your altar. Colour it in if you like, or use card and paint it gold, black or another colour of your choice.

Thursday

Mantra magic!

I radiate good witch vibes only

Friday

Cookie cutter spell

Make cookie dough. When you're mixing it, connect to the power of the four elements and imagine them flowing through you into the cookie mix. Cut into suns, moons and stars if you have shaped cookie cutters, or use a knife. Bake and enjoy eating your empowered magic cookies!

Saturday

Lucky stone spell

If you find a nice flat stone at the beach or on a walk, take it home and draw a pentagram or other magic symbol on it. Keep it on your altar, place around your home for protection or make it fancy and give as a gift!

Sunday

Mantra magic!

I am always true to myself

Week 50

Monday

Chilli wreath for a warm home

String a number of fresh red or green hot chillies on to some string with a needle (go through the green stalk and be careful when handling the chillies). Hang these up in your home to promote warmth and well-being.

Tuesday

Wish on a leaf spell

If you're out on a nature walk, find a nice big leaf that has already fallen from the tree and write a wish on it. You can release it to the wind or burn it when you get home.

Wednesday

Easy rose-petal-beauty tea spell

Collect rose petals and dry them. When dry, infuse in hot water, let them steep in a teapot and then drink (you might want to use a tea strainer when you pour). Rose promotes beauty and is also delicious as a tea!

Thursday

Mantra magic!

I call upon the universe to guide me to abundance

Friday

Imbolc ritual

To perform a ritual inspired by Imbolc – the celebration of the first stirrings of new life – begin by lighting two white candles and putting some flowers on your altar. If you're feeling crafty, make a Brigid's Cross – St Brigid is associated with Imbolc, and her four-armed cross represents luck, protection and abundance. When you have made the cross, place it on your altar and meditate on the coming of spring and what you plan to achieve. You could also plan a new creative project or ask the universe for creative inspiration. When you're finished, display the cross above your door or in a window for luck.

There are eight important dates for every witch's diary. Imbolc – the celebration of the first stirrings of new life – is celebrated on 1 February. In the northern hemisphere, white snowdrop flowers appear in gardens when the light starts to return. Imbolc is traditionally a fire festival associated with the reignited flame of creativity – a perfect to time to feel enthusiastic about a new creative project.

Saturday

Ostara ritual

To acknowledge the themes of polarity and balance at the Equinox, do a walking meditation. Mark out a spiral on your floor (or in your garden if you have one). You can use bird seed for outdoors so that the birds will remove it for you when you're done, something like dried peas or pebbles inside, or draw it in chalk if you can. Make the spiral at least a couple of metres in diameter – more, if you have the room.

Ostara is another name for the spring equinox. An equinox is the time of year when the length of days and nights are equal. At the spring equinox, we celebrate spring and new life – bunnies and eggs are familiar symbols of fertility at this time – but we also celebrate the perfect balance of the light and the dark.

Sunday

Mantra magic!

I am a magnet for positivity

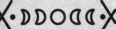

Week 51

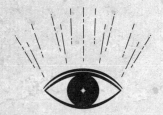

Monday

Beltane ritual

To harness the fertility of nature, make a flower crown! Find some seasonal flowers and weave them together into a circlet that will fit your head. You can add ribbons too if you like. Wear your crown to dance and give thanks for the bounty in your life, or have a Beltane party with your friends with fizzy drinks, sweet treats and lots of dancing!

Beltane is the time of year when Nature is at her most fertile and we celebrate her beautiful bounty. Beltane is also a fire festival, which has its roots in communities building bonfires throwing raucous parties to celebrate the growing crops. It occurs 1 May, and the vibe is eat, drink and be merry. Celebrate the abundance in your life!

Tuesday

Litha ritual

There are a lot of legends that talk about faeries spiriting foolish revellers away on the summer solstice, so leave an offering out for your local fae folk at Litha. In an outside space, you can leave a little bowl of milk or cream, some honey and flowers for the fae, and thank them for their presence. It's a good idea to do this regularly especially in your garden, if you have one, as it pays to stay on the faeries' good side

Litha – also known as the summer solstice – is the longest day in the northern hemisphere. It occurs 20–22 June, depending on the year, and is the day with the most daylight hours. Therefore, Litha is a celebration of the Sun and all it represents: life, success and joy. At the solstice, celebrate light and be thankful for all your successes.

Wednesday

Lughnasadh ritual

Lughnasadh celebrates the harvest, so what better way to mark the occasion than baking bread? You could add olives, nuts or fruits too, if you like. When you have prepared your dough, plait it into a loaf. As you plait it, give thanks for your year so far and all the things you have achieved. Bake and share with your friends!

Lughnasadh (also known as Lammas) occurs on 1 August and marks the ripeness of the crops in the fields – specifically wheat and grains. It is the first of two harvest festivals, where we start to reap what we have sown in the year. At Lughnasadh witches prepare a good meal, give thanks for what they have achieved so far and enjoy nature, perhaps with a walk.

Thursday

Mantra magic!

I trust the universe to provide me with all that I need in life

Friday

Mabon ritual

Make your own seasonal autumn potpourri to make your space smell lovely. Break up cinnamon sticks, dried apples, dry rosemary, dry orange peel and cloves with a mortar and pestle and add a couple of drops of vanilla or cinnamon oil. Add to a bowl on your altar and dress your altar with autumn leaves. This ritual can be enjoyed year-round.

Mabon is the autumn equinox – usually occurring 21–23 September, depending on the year – when the length of the days and nights in the northern hemisphere are equal. It is also traditionally the time of the second harvest for farmers, who would draw in their apples, squashes and grapes among other fruits and vegetables. Mabon is a good time to set intentions regarding ending things that aren't working for you: unhealthy habits or beliefs, perhaps.

Saturday

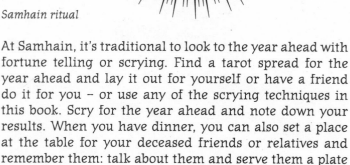

Samhain ritual

At Samhain, it's traditional to look to the year ahead with fortune telling or scrying. Find a tarot spread for the year ahead and lay it out for yourself or have a friend do it for you – or use any of the scrying techniques in this book. Scry for the year ahead and note down your results. When you have dinner, you can also set a place at the table for your deceased friends or relatives and remember them: talk about them and serve them a plate of food too. You could also put a photo of a dead relative or friend on your altar to remember them.

For witches, Samhain is the end of the Wheel of the Year, with the beginning of the witch's new year on 1 November. At Samhain, it is believed that the divide between our world and the underworld is at its thinnest, meaning that it's a time to remember the dead and journey into the underworld ourselves to reach our inner wisdom.

Sunday

Mantra magic!

My life is just beginning

Week 52

Monday

Yule ritual

In the UK we already tend to celebrate Yule as Christmas, in terms of putting up a tree and dressing it, eating special food such as a Yule log or a Christmas cake. A more witchy take on the winter solstice is to add oranges and burn frankincense on an altar and write down everything you want to release. When you have your list, burn it safely in your cauldron or other fire safe place, and enjoy a healthy and hearty meal.

At Yule, the winter solstice, we celebrate the return of the Sun. The winter solstice is the shortest day of the year when there are the most hours of darkness of any day of the year. It usually occurs around 21 December. Therefore, at Yule, we remember that even in the depths of darkness, there is hope, and that life will return.

Tuesday

Social media profile spell

To give your interactions on social media more pizazz, add an image of a pentagram or other magical symbol to your profile picture. Alternatively, you could choose a planetary symbol that resonates with you. When uploading your new image, ask the universe to bring good luck and protection to you.

Wednesday

Two palm comparison reading

It's said that your left hand represents the potential you were born with and your right hand represents what you made of that potential in life so far. Compare your life, love and fate lines on both hands (look them up online to see which is which) – is there potential you haven't yet explored? Are the lines very different on both hands or more or less the same?

Thursday

Mantra magic!

I am the main character in my own life

Friday

Knitting needles

You might not think that knitting (or crochet) is very witchy, but in fact both crafts can be very effective as spells. For any spell, choose a relevant colour wool for the outcome you want (pink for love, yellow for friendship, green for money, blue for luck, etc.) and source either knitting needles or a crochet hook. Every time you make a stitch, repeat a short spell you can make up in accordance with your goal. For instance, 'Money be mine' or 'Luck, come to me'. The repetition here is what makes the spell work, and you can work on your knitting or crochet until the outcome you want comes to you.

Saturday

Text/instant message love spell

Our friendships need frequent attention to thrive, and one of the best things you can do for your friends is to tell them you love them! On a Friday (Friday is the day of Venus, the planet of love), send a text or even a group message to the loved ones in your life with a big heart gif or whatever image representing love that you like best. Write your message of love in your own way, and then, before you press send, draw a pentagram and a heart in the air over your phone screen with a lit incense stick, three times each, so that you trace the shapes with the smoke. Say aloud 'Message of love, blessed from above' and send.

Sunday

Mantra magic!

I am grateful for all the good witch energy in my life

Spells for New Year's Eve and Leap Day

Twelve wishes spell

A new year is a chance to start afresh, and this spell will call in auspicious energies for the year ahead. Cast your circle, then place four candles – one at each compass point – on your altar and light them. Grab a piece of paper and write down twelve wishes for the coming year. Write the wishes as though they have already been achieved: I have a new best friend, I have aced my exams, for example. When you have finished, watch the flames dance before speaking your wishes aloud. Now roll up your paper and tie with string or a ribbon. Blow out your candles and wave the paper over the smoking candles.

Leap day ritual

Leap days are rare and special, so the magical energy around these days can be particularly potent. Use a leap day as a chance to commit to a long-term goal. You will need a small fabric bag, a needle and thread and an oak tree. Sit with your back against an oak tree, pick up an oak leaf from the ground or ask the tree for a leaf before you pick one from its branches. Think about something you truly want to manifest and talk to the tree about it – trees are good listeners and will absorb your wishes and send them deep into the earth through their roots. Take out your needle and thread and sew small crosses on the leaf, while saying the words: 'With every stitch my wish is granted, so mote it be.' When you have finished decorating the leaf, place it in the bag and hang it from the tree. Thank the tree for its ancient wisdom and magic.

Farewell

The spells in this book are small sparks to ignite your way to becoming a good witch of the highest order. Like Wednesday, you are a work in progress and you are powerful. Use your new skills for good and to manifest your best life. Now go and make magic!

Notes

Notes

Notes